Tillich and World Religions
Encountering Other Faiths Today

Tillich and World Religions

Encountering Other Faiths Today

by
ROBISON B. JAMES

MERCER UNIVERSITY PRESS
Macon, Georgia USA
April 2003

ISBN 0-86554-818-8   MUP/H620

Tillich and World Religions.
Encountering Other Faiths Today.
Copyright ©2003
Mercer University Press, Macon GA USA
Produced in the United States of America

Library of Congress Cataloging-in-Publication Data

James, Robison B., 1931–
    Tillich and word religions : encountering other faiths today /
    by Robison B. James.
    p. cm.
Includes bibliographical references (p. 157) and indexes.
    ISBN 0-86554-818-8
    1. Tillich, Paul, 1886–1965.
    2. Christianity and other religions.
    I. Title.
BR 127 .J35 2003
261.2'092--dc21

                                        2002153195

Contents

PART ONE
Understanding Tillich's Theology

PART TWO
Finding the Best Attitudes
in Interreligious Encounters

PART THREE
Looking at the Objective, Doctrinal Side

Preface

Two purposes lie behind this book, one scholarly, one practical. It has required a bit of work to combine the two, but I have been unwilling to give up on either one. I hope my two objectives have been well and truly wed in what I have written, and there is one early sign that this is the case. At the end of this preface I come back to this early sign.

One of my two purposes is to advance seven original, scholarly proposals as to how we may understand and apply the thought of Paul Tillich, one of the very great thinkers of the last century.[1]

My practical purpose is to use these scholarly proposals as recommendations to a fairly broad readership. Out of the wealth of Tillich's thinking, I recommend certain insights and attitudes that I believe will be of value as all of us engage in something that is becoming more and more common—"encountering other faiths today," in the words of this book's subtitle.

The audience to whom I make these recommendations includes at least these three subaudiences: (1) educated lay people who are interested in religion; (2) religion scholars, both those who know much about Tillich and those who know not so much; and (3) college and graduate students in courses that deal with Tillich and/or with the subject matter of this book.

In trying to reach these audiences, I take courage from the example of Paul Tillich himself. In 1959, his picture appeared on the cover of *Time* magazine.[2] He is one of the few theologians ever to appear there. One reason he was recognized in this way is that, in the heyday of his influence in the United States, from the early 1950s until his death in 1965, he reached the three audiences I envision for this book. At least this was the case with his shorter

---

[1]See the first note in the introduction, below.

[2]He was depicted on the cover of the 16 March 1959 issue. Wilhelm and Marion Pauck, *Paul Tillich: His Life and Thought*, vol. 1, *Life* (New York: Harper & Row, 1976) 269.

books, such as *Dynamics of Faith*,[3] and with his countless public addresses. I myself attended two of these general-audience lectures in 1958, and I can testify that he "connected" with his audience.[4]

Of the seven proposals put forward in this book, the most original is probably the way I bring together two things for the first time: (a) Tillich's analysis of three different depths of our experience; and (b) three attitudes that are distinguished in a typology that is familiar today, but was unknown in Tillich's time.[5]

According to (a) Tillich's analysis, we encounter religions either at a deep, existential level of experience, at a middle level of empathy and understanding, or at a detached and theoretical level. According to (b) the typology, when we size up religions other than "our own"—or other than the religion with which we are most familiar—we adopt one or the other of three attitudes. We adopt either an *exclusivist*, an *inclusivist*, or a *pluralist* attitude. I explain these attitudes in the introduction, below.

The proposal that appears to be most original is also the most basic to the book. I present it in chapter 4, "Rethinking the Typology of Pluralism, Inclusivism, and Exclusivism." On that Tillichian basis I begin in that same chapter the job of overhauling the threefold typology, and I continue this task in chapters 4–7, the four chapters that make up part two of the book.

This second part of the book, which many readers probably will feel is the heart of the book, is entitled "Finding the Best Attitudes in Interreligious Encounters." There I make four original

---

[3]Paul Tillich, *Dynamics of Faith* (New York: Harper & Row, 1957) now in a beautiful and inexpensive Perennial Classics Edition, with an introduction by Tillich biographer Marion Pauck (New York: Perennial/HarperCollins Publishers Inc., 2001).

[4]Paul Tillich, "The Present Encounter of World Religions," and "The Present Encounter of Religious and Secular Faiths," unpublished Wesley Lectures delivered in Chapel Hill, North Carolina, 3 and 4 October 1958. Notes by Robison B. James in his personal files.

[5]This is the first and most basic of a number of differences between the present work and another that has not been very well received, namely, Terence Thomas's 1983 dissertation at the University of Notthingham, now published as Terence Thomas, *Paul Tillich and World Religions* (Fairwater, Cardiff, Wales: Cardiff Academic Press, 1999).

proposals, five proposals altogether. I summarize them at the end of chapter 7. Here I need only say that I include among these proposals the suggestion that we can adopt and should adopt, not just one of the three attitudes, but a reconceived version of *each* of them.

In the last two chapters of the book, 8 and 9, the focus shifts from our attitudes to a somewhat more outward-looking perspective. These chapters constitute part three of the book, "Looking at the Objective, Doctrinal Side." Each presents one more of my proposals.

Chapter 8 proposes that we find in Tillich's thought an almost explicit argument of considerable force and subtlety. It is a two-step argument that the Christian message has the "strongest" credentials for becoming the universal faith of humankind—"strongest" in the sense that the symbolic core of the Christian message has the least imperialistic and most self-surrendering thrust of any religion that offers salvation through and within our historical experience.

The somewhat doctrinal focus of chapter 8 continues in chapter 9, but this final chapter also marks a change from the rest of the volume. Until I get to chapter 9, I am for the most part working out what I find to be useful in Tillich's thought. The ideas are Tillichian, and one would think I was a Tillichian, as well. I have often been mistaken for such.[6]

However, in chapter 9 I propose a significant change in Tillich's "model of reality," that is, in his ontology. I propose to build into Tillich's basic ontological structure something that it demonstrably lacks, the "I-Thou" categories we find in the great Jewish (and very biblical) thinker, Martin Buber. What is proposed in that chapter is a decidely *revisionist* Tillichianism.

---

[6]Some eight years ago, after decades of scholarly exchanges with Prof. Lewis Ford concerning convergences and contrasts between Tillich and Alfred North Whitehead (see the acknowledgements, below), Lewis was stunned when I said I had very basic disagreements with Tillich. I had told him about them long before, but he had long since forgotten or assumed I did not continue to hold them.

The last of my seven original proposals is both unfriendly and friendly toward Tillich's thought. It is unfriendly in the sense that I try to show precisely why Tillich's God is not sufficiently personal, at least for many of us who are beholden to the Christian Scriptures. But that last proposal is friendly insofar as it suggests that even those who disagree with something quite basic in Tillich may nevertheless employ much of his wisdom and insight.

In the last place, I want to say something now about the first of my seven proposals. In chapters 2 and 3, I argue and explain the following proposal: for many purposes, and perhaps for most purposes, we can better understand "how Tillich's theology works" if we see it as a synthesis of "dialectics" and "paradox" than as a product of Tillich's "method of correlation." I explain in chapters 2 and 3 what these terms mean.

I am not so foolish as to think Tillich was mistaken about how his own theology was put together. He was not mistaken on this point; and I sense some strategic and tactical reasons why, given the situation he addressed, he was probably wise to structure his theology as he did. And it is quite correct to say that it *correlates* our real-life questions with the powerfully symbolic answers given in the Christian message. But what Tillich is doing can be described in other ways—in ways that make the moving parts and interconnections of his system stand out with greater clarity than does the rather clumsy notion of "correlation."[7]

At this point, once again, my practical purpose in this book comes into play. Chapters 2 and 3 are not only intended to advance the scholarly proposal I have just described. They are also meant to introduce Tillich's theology to *Tillich novices*, that is, to readers who know little or nothing about his thought. The idea is, if we are to use Tillich's theology in the rest of the book, we should try to "get the hang of it" at the outset. Thus, part one of the book—that is, chapters 2 and 3—is called "Understanding Tillich's Theology."

In order to combine my second with my first purpose in chapters 2 and 3, I have done two things. First, I have confined my

---

[7]See Tillich's own explication of "The Method of Correlation," ST 1:59-66, esp. 60.

scholarly debates to the footnotes. General readers perhaps need not read my footnotes in any case, but even those inclined to read footnotes may wish, by contrast, to avoid the *long* notes in chapters 2 and 3—though I hope scholars will love them. Most of the short notes should not be much of a menace in these and other chapters.

Second, I have submitted these chapters to three qualified readers—"qualified" in the sense that they were novices. They knew little about Tillich. My chapters "passed." These readers found them intelligible. They also made a dozen suggestions for additional clarity, and I have incorporated all their suggestions into a major rewriting of the chapters.

Although this is an early sign that my scholarly and practical purposes are happily married, I am well aware that the real test lies ahead. In that test, I cannot promise an easy read, and certainly not a bedtime read. But I think I can promise something else. Especially if the general reader will bring a bit of persistence to bear, the results should not only be worth the effort, but that and much more.

Acknowledgments

Scholarship lives and grows in settings where ideas and papers are exchanged. During the decade in which this book has been gestating, I have been fortunate to have enjoyed six such circles of friends and colleagues. The first of these is the richly varied annual meetings of the North American Paul Tillich Society, an organization of which I was president in 2001–2002. The second is the stimulating annual meetings of a group in the American Academy of Religion that is currently named "Paul Tillich: Issues in Theology, Culture, and Religion," a panel of which I am 2001–2006 cochair with Professor Mary Ann Stenger of the University of Louisville.

Thirdly, there is the biennial "International Paul Tillich Symposium" in Frankfurt/Main, Germany, the guiding and supporting spirit for which is Bishop Gert Hummel, formerly professor at the University of Saarbrücken, and now Lutheran bishop in the Republic of Georgia. The omnicompetent person who makes the details of Bishop Hummel's symposia happen is Doris Lax, of Bruchmühlbach, Germany. Her doctoral work on Tillich's thought has made her a valued scholarly colleague as well as a translator of some of my articles.

A fourth venue for me was a seminar on Tillich's theology in the summer semester of 2000 at the University of Heidelberg, a venture I co-led with Peter Haigis, without whose help at crisis moments, my German would not have sufficed.

A fifth and sixth venue have forced me to understand what I can in French, though I was allowed to write and speak in English. The first of these is the biennial meetings of the Association Paul Tillich d'Éxpression Française, now under the presidency of Prof. Marc Boss of the Institut Protestant de Théologie, Montpellier, France. The second is a series of sessions held at the University of Laval under the leadership of Prof. Jean Richard, director of a multiyear Tillich translation and interpretation project there. In August 2002, I gave a preview of this book at one of these sessions, and received valuable feedback. Jean Richard has

provided encouragement to my Tillich scholarship for years—
sometimes out of the blue like a gift from God.

Three colleagues, two of them already named, have devoted
generous amounts of time to working over earlier versions of
certain parts of this volume. For the way I now formulate and
clarify the chief ideas in chapters 2 and 3, and for some of the
substance of those ideas, I am much indebted to a remarkable
eight-month series of exchanges during 1999–2000 with Marc Boss.
In a series of long footnotes in those chapters, I detail our debates,
and our near agreement if not our complete agreement, on Tillich's
developing idea of "paradox," on the relation between essentialism
and existentialism in Tillich, and on what Tillich thought he owed
to Nicholas of Cusa.

Jean Richard ably translated into French a long article that was
an earlier version of part two of this book, chapters 4–7; and as he
did so he prompted me not only to clarify my English but also to
expand and correct several of my concepts, especially on the
relations between "inclusivism" and "pluralism." Similarly, though
in a more localized way, Prof. John J. Thatamanil of Millsaps
College looked over portions of these same four chapters and
caused me to rethink and make changes on the subjects of multiple
religious identities, mysticism, and "exclusivism versus pluralism."

It almost goes without saying that any remaining inadequacies
in this book are mine alone, and that none of the three scholars
named should be assumed to agree with what I say.

I must also acknowledge a debt to three bright persons who
had never studied Tillich. They were willing to be my "guinea
pigs" for chapters 2 and 3, which I intend to be both a beginner's
introduction to Tillich *and* a scholarly proposal. They found the
chapters intelligible (except for the footnotes, which they were not
supposed to read). At my request, they made extensive suggestions
for further clarity, all of which I have incorporated into a total
rewriting. They are Sara James Butcher of New York City, and
John and Elizabeth James Gallagher of San Ramon, California.
They are now family in an added sense.

The understanding of Paul Tillich that underlies this book has
long roots that should also be put on the record. Prof. A. Durwood
Foster, now emeritus at Pacific School of Religion, got me started

in a graduate course on Tillich at Duke University in 1958. He still suffers patiently my spirited disagreements with Tillich, which now go hand in hand with my profound appropriation, not just my appreciation, of much of Tillich's wisdom.

The person who got me started on my doctoral dissertation, "The Symbolic Knowledge of God in the Theology of Paul Tillich" (Duke University, 1965), was the late Prof. Robert E. Cushman, although within a couple of weeks of doing so he became dean of the Duke Divinity School. Thereupon, the late Prof. Frederick Herzog became and happily remained my official "Doctor Father," although it was the late Prof. Charles K. Robinson of Duke who provided me direction during the last months of work, while Herzog was on leave.

Since the 1960s, when he also was completing a dissertation on Tilllich, I have been involved in unceasing conversations and written exchanges with Prof. Lewis S. Ford, editor of *Process Studies* 1971–1996, and now emeritus of Old Dominion University. The challenge for me in these exchanges was to rethink and restate a wide range of Tillich's doctrines so that they might be more telling for one whose heart was always with Alfred North Whitehead, not Tillich. Someday we may yet do our Tillich-Whitehead book.

My students at the University of Richmond during several decades and now, since 2000, my students at the Baptist Theological Seminary at Richmond have helped me to understand things in Tillich in ways that sometimes surprised me. They also have a knack for showing how relevant much of his thought is, and occasionally how relevant some of it is *not*—or not until it is recontextualized, in any case.

Chapters 2 and 3 are a massive rewriting of my "Mystical Identity and Acceptance 'In Spite Of': Paul Tillich as a Synthesis of Cusanus and Luther."[8]

Chapters 4–7 are a thorough revision and expansion of the English that underlies my "La rencontre interreligieuse d'après

---

[8]In *Mystisches Erbe in Tillichs philosophischer Theologie*, Proceedings of the VIII International Paul-Tillich Symposium, Frankfurt/Main 2000, Tillich-Studien 3, ed. Gert Hummel and Doris Lax (Münster, Hamburg, London: LIT-Verlag, 2000) 164-76.

Paul Tillich: pour une nouvelle conception de l'exclusivism, de l'inclusivism et du pluralisme."[9] A more remote ancestor of chapters 4–7 is "Tillich on 'the Absoluteness of Christianity.' "[10]

With many changes and additions, chapter 9 is based upon parts of my "Revising Tillich's Model of Reality to Add Buber's I-Thou."[11]

To all those named, and many others whom I dare not begin to name, I can only say my appreciation is unbounded, my affection unflagging.

---

[9]Trans. Jean Richard, in *Laval Philosophique et Theologique* (Québec) 58 (2002): 43-64. The same article appears also in the proceedings of the May 2001 annual meeting of the French-speaking Tillich society in Marseille, France (Münster: LIT Verlag, 2002).

[10]In *Papers from the Annual Meeting of the North American Paul Tillich Society, Philadelphia PA, November 1995*, ed. Robert P. Scharlemann (Charlottesville VA.: North American Paul Tillich Society, 1997) 35-50.

[11]In *Being versus Word in Tillich's Theology?*, Proceedings of the International Paul Tillich Symposium, Frankfurt/Main, 1998, ed. Gert Hummel (Berlin and New York: Walter de Gruyter, 1999) 237-48.

Abbreviations

GW   *Gesammelte Werke.* Edited by Renate Albrecht. Fourteen
       volumes. Stuttgart: Evangelisches Verlagswerk, 1959–1990.

MW   *Main Works / Hauptwerke.* Edited by Carl Heinz Ratschow
       with the collaboration of John Clayton, Gert Hummel,
       Erdmann Sturm, Michael Palmer, Robert P. Scharlemann,
       and Gunther Wenz. Six volumes. Berlin/New York: de
       Gruyter—Evangelisches Verlagswerk GmbH, 1987–1998.

ST   *Systematic Theology.* Three volumes. Chicago: University of
       Chicago Press, 1951, 1957, 1963.

Chapter 1

Introduction

Although Paul Tillich (1886–1965) is widely recognized as one of the most important theologians of the last century,[1] and although there is also some evidence of a revival of interest in his thought,[2] neither of these things inspired the writing of this book. If I explain how the idea for the book originated, I do so because that may make it clear how significant some of Tillich's ideas are for the questions with which this book grapples.

---

[1]Paul Tillich's writings still appear regularly in syllabi and on reading lists in courses in theology and religious studies. Organized groups of scholars in a half-dozen countries continue to study, interpret, and make use of his thought. These groups include the North American Paul Tillich Society; the American Academy of Religion's group now entitled "Tillich: Issues in Theology, Religion and Culture" (newly reestablished in 2002); the Association Paul Tillich d'Éxpression Française (in France, Québec, and Switzerland); the biennial International Paul Tillich Symposia in Frankfurt/Main, Germany; the flourishing Deutsche Paul Tillich Gesellschaft; and the Tillich societies in the Netherlands and Brazil.

[2]In addition to what I say in the preceding note—especially the fact that the American Academy of Religion's program committee revived the AAR Tillich group in 2002—I may point to four publication programs. (1) Since 1990 a project has been under way to translate Tillich into French. The codirectors are Prof. Jean Richard, University of Laval, Québec, and Prof. André Gounelle, Institut Protestant de Théologie, Montpellier, France. As of 2003, seven of Tillich's most important ouvre had been published jointly by Les Éditions du Cerf (Paris), Éditions Labor et Fides (Geneva), and Les Presses de l'Université Laval (Québec). The rest of Tillich's main works are expected to follow in a few years. (2) Beginning in 1999, LIT Verlag of Münster, Germany launched *Tillich Studien*, a series of works on the life and thought of Tillich. By 2003, eight volumes had appeared under the coeditorship of Prof. Werner Schüssler of the University of Trier and Prof. Erdmann Sturm of the University of Münster. (3) For the last several years, approximately two books per year on Tillich have been published by Mercer University Press, and the next years are expected to be similar. And (4) in November 2002, the North American Paul Tillich Society launched its "Tillich Collected Works Project" with me as chair.

I. Inspiration for the Book

In 1992, I had for decades been holding two oil-and-water things together in my mind, and sometimes talking about them together as well. I felt a good bit of tension between the two things, but I thought I had found a way to hold them together that was rather astute, and also rather original.

The first of these oil-and-water things was my feeling that, if people hold any religion as their ultimate concern, and if their religion means something positive to them, then their faith is bound to be something they will wish to share with others if others are interested, and if the conditions are right (for example, if the situation is free of duress such as the poor grade a teacher might give a student). Insofar as I was a Christian, this first thing was a belief that the mission of sharing its message belongs to the essence of Christianity; and that meant, in turn, that taking part in such a mission belongs in the life of any serious adherent of the faith, even if the adherent did nothing more than provide financial support for the Christian mission.

In addition to this sense of mission, however, the other thing I was holding together in my thought and speech was an openness for other faiths. It was a large and constantly growing appreciation for the remarkable spirituality, saintliness, and goodness of some persons of other faiths (plus some people of secular "faiths"), and my growing appreciation, likewise, for the profundity and transforming power I sensed in other religions at their best, and in some nonreligious ultimate concerns at *their* best.

I do not want to provide an explanation here as to how I was holding these two things together. That would get ahead of the story I want to tell in this book.[3] But I do want to say something about the *origin* of the "rather astute" way I was managing to do this.

---

[3] I will say now, using terms to be explained later, that people can find a sense of mission nurtured and expressed by a "contextually exclusivist" attitude, and that they can find their openness to other faiths undergirded by two other attitudes they can also adopt—"reciprocal inclusivism" and "contextual pluralism"—as well as by the fact that their exclusivism is *only* contextual.

It was in 1992, as I say, and I was rereading most of the disser-tation I had written decades earlier on Tillich's thought. (Some people actually do that!) The realization that dawned upon me during that rereading was as follows. My rather astute and supposedly original ideas for holding together a sense of mission and an openness toward other faiths were insights I had absorbed decades earlier as I researched and wrote that dissertation.[4] I had reworked the insights in my own way. A few of the fingerprints on them were mine. But Tillich's fingerprints were all over those insights. And I was well aware who got there first.

These astute ideas are the nucleus of this book, or of parts two and three of the book, in any case. To be sure, this nucleus is now much enlivened by fresh encounters with Tillich, and much elabo-rated. As I try to make clear, I not infrequently elaborate and apply Tillich's ideas beyond the point at which he left them at his death.

2. Interreligious Encounters Today

There is an *occasion* for this book as well as a nucleus and inspira-tion for it. The occasion is something that has been gathering strength for a long time in the United States and other Western countries. The horrifying events in the United States on September 11, 2001 only made unmistakable for many what had long been obvious to some. Encounters with "other faiths" have been increasing in frequency and importance in Western countries for at least thirty years. Despite the centrality of the Christian tradition in much of Western culture, these lands have become so religiously diverse within, and so globally interconnected without, that the only way we inhabitants of these lands can avoid interreligious encounters is to "drop out" and lose touch with our environment.

I shall say more about what I mean by "interreligious encoun-ters" in a moment. Suffice it to say that the tragic events just mentioned, though they are a glaring example, are a rare and poor example of the genre.

---

[4]Robison Brown James, "The Symbolic Knowledge of God in the Theology of Paul Tillich" (Ph.D. diss., Duke University, 1965).

If we take the United States as a test case, we can immediately see what has been happening by placing two textbooks on American religion side by side. Perhaps the standard when it was published in 1972 was Sydney Ahlstrom's *A Religious History of the American People*.[5] It is massively centered in Christianity, devoting otherwise only some forty of its eleven hundred pages to Judaism.

By contrast, a considerable "decentering" has taken place in a work that had become a choice textbook by the 1990s, namely, Catherine L. Albanese's *America: Religions and Religion*.[6] She gives substantial attention to the following traditions, among others: native American traditions and the Hinduism, Buddhism, and Islam that are found in the United States.

Particularly insofar as Islam, Buddhism, and Hinduism are concerned, we may also take note of the "Pluralism Project" directed by Diana L. Eck of Harvard,[7] and her summation of some of the results of that project in a book published in 2001. The book bears the provocative full title of *A New Religious America: How a "Christian Country" Has Now Become the World's Most Religiously Diverse Nation*.[8]

It will be clear what I mean by "interreligious encounters" if I explain that they can happen in dozens of ways. For example, we may come into casual or social contact with persons whose religious backgrounds are different from ours. We may visit a religious observance of some "other religion." We may read an article or view a television program about "another religion." We may be confronted in a news story with an unfamiliar religion, or

---

[5]Sydney Ahlstrom, *A Religious History of the American People* (New Haven CT: Yale University Press, 1972).

[6]The book was being advertised in 2002 in its third edition of 1998. Only the first edition has been available to me, namely, Catherine L. Albanese, *America: Religions and Religion* (Belmont CA.: Wadsworth Publishing Co., 1981). See also four articles on the theme, "Is There a Center to American Religious History," *Church History: Studies in Christianity and Culture* 71 (June 2002): 368-90.

[7]"PluralismProject,"<http://www.fas.harvard.edu/~pluralism/index.html>. Accessed 26 August 2002.

[8]Diana L. Eck, *A New Religious America: How a "Christian Country" Has Now Become the World's Most Religiously Diverse Nation* (San Francisco: HarperSanFrancisco, 2001).

with the impact of that religion upon some country or some train of events. Or we may deliberately engage in dialogue with people of a contrasting faith.

Part two of this book is concerned with encounters of the kind just illustrated. In those four chapters, as I explain in the preface, we seek to find the best attitudes for such experiencs of interreligious encounter.

But it is also an interreligious encounter when we puzzle or wonder how "our faith" or "our nonfaith" relates to "other religions," or when we inquire about the contrasts that are to be found among various religions. In such encounters we look at the more objective, doctrinal differences, rather than adopting this or that attitude toward a faith or perspective different from our own.

Part three of this book selects two interreligious encounters of this second kind to deal with. As we have seen in the preface, chapter 8 deals with the features of a religion that make it most apt to be a universal faith for humankind. And chapter 9 deals with the great contrast in religions between a personal and an impersonal understanding of God or of Ultimate Reality.

My mention of "other religions" in the preceding paragraph prompts me to say something for readers of this book who adhere to no particular religion. Whenever I speak about "our religion" or the like, these readers should take me to mean "the religion that is *most familiar* to them." And whenever I use such expressions as "another religion," these readers should take me to mean "any religion *other* than the one with which they are most familiar."[9]

3. A Famous Typology and Tillich

One tool for dealing with such interreligious encounters has been available for more than twenty years. It is the typology I mention in the preface.[10] According to this typology, we adopt one or the

---

[9]It is contrary to my purpose to "leave anyone out." Also, on grounds of Tillich's thought—if I may now shift to the broader sense in which Tillich uses the term—even secular people have a "religion" or its equivalent. People's "ultimate concerns" are their religions (ST 1:11-15, 211).

[10]For all practical purposes, the typology originated with Alan Race, *Christians and Religious Pluralism* (Maryknoll NY: Orbis, 1982) 71, 94-97.

other of three different attitudes toward "other religions."[11] (1) If we adopt a "pluralist" attitude, we say that each of the *plural* world religions possesses religious or transforming truth that is just as valid, effective, and valuable as any of the others. (2) If we adopt an "inclusivist" attitude, we say that the standard for all saving truth is given in "my" religion, but other religions *include* more or less of that truth and power. (3) If we adopt an "exclusivist" attitude, we say that religious or saving truth is found *exclusively* in our own religion.

Some problems have been detected in this typology. As it is customarily employed, it assumes that salvation is ultimately the same thing in all faiths. That is empirically wrong. And in the way it has often been employed, the typology can also get tangled up in some conceptual incoherence. In particular, pluralists often turn out to be either inclusivists or exclusivists, despite themselves.[12]

However, I believe we can view these flaws as "mere technical problems." For one thing, we are not forced to use the typology in the way it has usually been employed. In any case, I find that the typology works reasonably well, up to a point. Many of us find that we really are more comfortable with one of the three attitudes than we are with the others. And we sometimes find ourselves ready to argue with people who champion one of the other attitudes, if not *both* of those other attitudes.

---

[11]I may perhaps refer once more to what I say above about readers of this book who adhere to no religion. For them, "other religions" are any religions except the one with which they are most familiar.

[12]Pluralistis take their own understanding of the way various religions embody salvation—they take their own "faith"—to be the deepest wisdom on that subject. They then tacitly assume or openly affirm one of the following propositions. Either they say none of the religious traditions possesses that deep wisdom, and in that case the would-be pluralists are exclusivists. Or, alternatively, pluralists say that various religious traditions approach their own (the pluralists') faith and wisdom more or less closely, and in this latter case the would-be pluralists are inclusivists. See S. Mark Heim, *Salvations* (Maryknoll NY: Orbis, 1995) 4-7 and chap. 5; and J. A. DiNoia, *The Diversity of Religions* (Washington DC: Catholic University of America, 1992) esp. 47-55, "Beyond Exclusivism, Inclusivism, and Pluralism."

The major problem I find with the typology is of another kind. My complaint with it is that it tells us, in effect, that we can only be one of the three things, an exclusivist, a pluralist, or an inclusivist. I do not think that is right, and it is at least in part some Tillichian insights that make me think that. It seems to me that a lot of us tend to be two of these things at different times, if not all three of them at different times. And we can sometimes be two or more of these things *almost* at the same time.

However, the moment we decide to loosen up the typology so that we can be both inclusivist and exclusivist, or both inclusivist and pluralist, for example, things tend to become very confused. It soon gets difficult to figure out how this all works in real life.

This is where Tillich comes to the rescue. Precisely how Tillich can offer help is hinted at above, in the preface; but the help we derive from him is what part two of this book is all about. As already noted, I summarize the results at the end of chapter 7.

4. Part Three of the Book and Evangelicals' Potential Use of Tillich

Both the chapter titles in part three of this book and the way I preview them in the preface suggest that Tillich should be of considerable interest to a religious community that ordinarily has little to do with Paul Tillich. I refer to the community of evangelicals. Or I refer to the goodly fellowship of evangelical theologians, in any case.

These theologians could hardly be uninterested in an argument that the Christian message is more universal than others, or in an effort to make someone's idea of God—Tillich's, in this case—more "biblical" than it originally was. These are my goals, respectively, in chapters 8 and 9.

But I believe evangelical theologians may be at least equally interested in the argument I develop in part two of this book as a whole. This is most obviously the case in chapter 5, "Contextual Exclusivism." I title the third section of that chapter "Why Contextual Exclusivism Belongs in Evangelical Theology."

Lest the title of that section itself be misleading, I should be clear that, when I say contextual exclusivism belongs in evangelical theology, my view is that *only* a contextual kind of exclusivism belongs there. I am persuaded that a noncontextual or categorical kind of exclusivism is contrary to the witness of the Christian Scriptures themselves, although I cannot argue that point here.[13]

Inasmuch as I am making something of an overture here to evangelical theologians, and inasmuch as they understandably have reservations about Tillich—and also about any book dealing with Tillich's thought, as this one does—let me make a further point about what Tillich has to offer.

As he has been to others, Tillich was a great help to me in my understanding and appropriating some motifs in the Gospel of John and in Paul's letters. These New Testament motifs had been hidden from me by my Baptist-evangelical upbringing. I refer to such powerful ideas as what it means to "participate in Christ," which is more than simply having Christ inside one's individual heart, though that is part of it. The reason these corporate and somewhat mystical motifs had been hidden from me for years was that the evangelical outlook, as I now recognize, was riveted to a modern, quasi-Newtonian, individualistic worldview.[14]

Since a significant amount of Tillich's thought revolves around the early church fathers' appropriation of the New Testament witness, he is able to do something that the quite modern evangelical outlook does not allow to happen. Tillich opens up the corporate and somewhat mystical ideas of such figures as I have alluded to, Ireneus, Athanasius, and the Cappadocaians, not to mention Paul and John.

---

[13]I do not present a sustained argument for the point I have just made in this book, but I do provide at least two kinds of support for it. (1) On pp. 87-91 below, I seek to show that contextual exclusivism is "prophetic" in the sense of the central line of biblical faith. (2) In n. 28 on p. 88, I seek to show that Acts 4:12, supposedly an exclusivist text, is only *contextually* exclusivist—and that it is "contextually exclusivist" precisely in the prophetic or biblical sense.

[14]See my "The Modern Super-Acts Worldview," a self-published text in Christian Theology II, HT 2312, Baptist Theological Seminary at Richmond, Spring semester 2002. A refocused version of this essay is scheduled for the Southeast regional meeting in Chattanooga, Tenn., in March 2003, of the American Academy of Religion under the title "Reconciling Hermeneutics Right and Left in American Christianity by Dissolving the 'Conspiracy' betweem Newtonian and Book-of-Acts Ontologies." I epitomize the argument of this essay in n. 3 on p. 71, below.

Thus, if I may generalize from others' experience and from my own, when evangelicals decide fully to become what they are confident they already are, namely, "biblical thinkers" rather than "modernists," they could very well turn for help to Paul Tillich.[15]

To be sure, evangelical theologians can get the help that some of them need from other sources; and I readily acknowledge that they will also wish to avoid some things in Tillich, as I myself do as well.

5. Can Tillich Reconcile Liberals and Conservatives?

I have said that I aim for this book to be of practical use. There is one way it could be useful that I have only implicitly commented upon thus far. I believe the book suggests a way to resolve at least *some* of the conflicts and confusions among liberals, moderates, and conservatives over interreligious issues. When I say that, I have in mind the Christian community. Other religious traditions may not be affected by these conflicts and confusions, at least not with the same severity.

But certainly among a great many Christians there is a recurrent "syndrome" regarding interreligious issues. Conservatives veer toward a doctrinaire exclusivism that seems to know as much as God knows about who could possibly be recipients of divine grace; liberals tend to settle into a pluralism that can drain away passion and commitment; mellow moderates grope toward an inclusivism of some kind, sometimes unsure how to make their positions clear, much less how to make them convincing; and a lot of these people get mad at each other, at least off and on.

---

[15]Other places later in the book where I argue similar points are on p. 77, where I devote a long footnote (n. 3) to this same idea that Tillich can help evangelicals be more fully biblical, and also on pp. 131-33, 135, and 139-40. In the latter places I believe I show that the deep structure of Tillich's theology is a potent rendering of the deep eschatological structure of New Testament faith.

I might add that there is no contradiction between (a) our finding that the Tillichian deity is less personal than the biblical God (as I find to be the case—see chap. 9) and (b) our finding that Tillich can open up much of the Bible for evangelicals who are modernists despite themselves. The key idea is to view Tillich's pantheistic-tending deity (with some alterations, of course) as a rendering of the *immanent side* of the God who is both immanent and transcendent.

Here again Tillich can help. As I try to explain in the rest of the book, his thought points a way through these conflicts and confusions. It shows how there is a *lot* to be said for each of the three positions in the debate. And his thought shows how there is a *lot more* to be said for holding those three positions together—for holding them together in a grand perspective that reconceives and reconciles them all, and that just might be able to reconcile a lot of the people who get caught up in the syndrome I have tried to describe.

6. What to Read Next

The next two chapters in this book comprise the only part of the book, part one, that does not deal directly with interreligious issues. The role of these chapters, as is obvious, is to open up Tillich's theology so that one may make use of it in pursuing the interreligious issues.

The reader has a choice at this point, however. Chapters 2 and 3 should make the rest of the book more three-dimensional, and also easier to follow. But it is also quite possible to skip them and go directly to chapter 4. Most readers may simply follow their interests in this matter.

This holds also for "Tillich novices"—for those who have never studied Tillich. As noted in the preface, I have taken considerable pains to make my introduction to Tillich in the next two chapters something an educated Tillich novice can understand. Here, too, however, if these readers find they are bogging down, I would not hesitate to recommend that they jump to chapter 4. If that happens—although I do not think it will—I doubt it will happen before some place in chapter 3.

(If a reader does bog down, whether in chapter 3 or elsewhere, the index may prove helpful. It has been prepared with considerable care, and several of the key terms listed there have references to pages in the book where that term is "explained," or "described and illustrated," or the like. Often the pages marked "passim" will also serve this purpose.)

PART ONE

Understanding Tillich's Theology

Chapter 2

Keys to Tillichian Thought[1]

If we are to make use of Paul Tillich's thought to help us deal with the conflicts and confusions that arise from our encounters with other religions, we must obviously understand his theology.

How difficult is that? Is it possible to get a grip on Tillich in only a chapter or two? He has a reputation for being a profound thinker, and not easy to understand. Further, some people have felt—wrongly, as we shall see—that his thought is closer to being a series of fragments than a systematic whole.[2]

---

[1]In my acknowledgements, above, I state my indebtedness to Prof. Marc Boss of the Institut Protestant de Théologie, Montpellier, France, for his contribution to the way I have conceived this chapter and the next. My understanding of the relation between dialectics and paradox in Tillich dates to my doctoral dissertation (cited above and below, and in the bibliography), but I learned much from our exchanges in 1999–2000. In particular, I gained an enriched idea of "paradox." On that point, see n. 7 in the next chapter.

For such differences as may remain between us (if any) see nn. 7 and 11 in this chapter, and the last long note in the next chapter. We are certanly not as far apart as we thought we were when we wrote and revised the two following interacting papers: Robison B. James, "Mystical Identity and Acceptance 'In Spite Of': Paul Tillich as a Synthesis of Cusanus and Luther," referenced in the acknowledgments, above; and Marc Boss, "*Coincidentia oppositorum* und Rechtfertigung—das cusanische Erbe in Paul Tillichs Denken," *Mystisches Erbe in Tillichs philosophischer Theologie*, Proceedings of the VIII International Paul Tillich Symposium, Frankfurt/Main 2000, ed. Gert Hummel and Doris Lax, *Tillich Studien* 3 (Münster, Hamburg, London: LIT-Verlag, 2000) 135-63.

See also my dissertation, "The Symbolic Knowledge of God in the Theology of Paul Tillich" (Ph.D. diss., Duke University, 1965) 187-201.

[2]An example is the late Carl Heinz Ratschow (chief editor of the six-volume *Paul Tillich: Main Works/Hauptwerke*). He said there is no lasting body of systematic doctrine underlying the deft and methodical way Tillich dealt with different questions throughout his life. See his ninety-one-page introduction to a collection of Tillich's writings: Ratschow, "Einführung," in *Tillich Auswahl*, 3 vols., ed. Manfred Baumotte (Gütersloh: Gütersloher Verlagshaus Mohn, 1980) esp. 1:14-15, 18-20.

Ratschow's point is not convincing. In the same introduction he sets forth a significant core of ideas that, as he himself says, Tillich maintained throughout

However, *on one condition* I believe that all such supposed problems are nonissues and that, in thirty or forty pages of reading, literate people can learn how Tillich's systematic theology works. I also believe that, upon learning that much, one will find that Tillich sheds much light on the various religious situations in which we find ourselves—including those situations in which we come up against religions other than the one(s) with which we are most familiar.

The "one condition" of which I speak is that *we find the right keys to Tillich's theology.*

I. The Key Tillich Offers: Correlation

Of course, Tillich has himself provided us with a key to his theology, namely, "correlation." The fact that his three-volume *Systematic Theology* proceeds according to his "method of correlation" (ST 1:59-68) means that, one by one, Tillich takes up five deep yearnings or "questings" that belong to human existence itself. Then, since he is doing Christian theology, he "correlates" with each of these existential questions the answer that is given in the Christian message.

Tillich believes the answers provided by all religions to these existential questions come in symbolic terms. Thus his method, in a nutshell, is his interpreting what these answers mean by correlating certain existential questions with certain religious symbols.[3]

We can illustrate this by looking at two of the five existential questions in Tillich's system. (a) We are always concerned and sometimes anxious about where our lives are headed, and where the whole human story is headed. The Christian message offers

---

much or all of his professional life. Ratschow, "Einführung," 26, 32, 54, 57, 59, 72, 99-100. My own judgment is that Ratschow failed to find a lasting, systematic basis of doctrine in Tillich because, so far as one can tell from his introduction, he did not make use of Tillich's three main systematic works, early and late, *Das System der Wissenschaften* (1923), *Religionsphilosophie* (1925), and *Systematic Theology* (1951–1963). Cf. a 2300-word letter from me to Ratschow (letter of 22 June 1997 in my personal files).

[3]Cf. Tillich, "Existential Analyses and Religious Symbols" (1956), MW 6:385-400.

hope for the Kingdom of God and for Eternal Life. We have some precise ideas about what these two things are, and we should. But despite those ideas, we are aware that these two things are bigger, and that more is involved, than we can grasp in literal, exact terms. That is, the Kingdom of God and Eternal Life are symbolic. And that means they are more real, not less real, than the literal understandings we may have about what is involved.

(b) The second illustration is that we experience guilt and estrangement. We are always concerned and sometimes anxious about whether we are living as we should, and whether we are really "connected" with others, and with the God who is the basis and meaning of our lives. The Christian message offers reconciliation in "Jesus as the Christ," that is, in Jesus received as the one who brings salvation, and the whole age of salvation. Here again, despite the precise ideas we have about such things, we sooner or later realize that there is more to Jesus as Christ and Savior than flesh and blood can figure out. That is, "Jesus as the Christ" is symbolic, powerfully and transformingly so. Its significance has to be revealed by Jesus' "Father who is in heaven" (Matthew 16:17).

2. The Keys Proposed Here

Of course, I accept Tillich's "correlation" as an important key to his theology. Further, the principal key I propose here is fully consistent with "correlation." Nevertheless, I do not believe correlation is the only key, nor for all purposes the best key. In fact, I believe the principal key I propose helps to explain correlation, and to make it more intelligible.[4]

Thus, as the principal key to unlock Tillich's theology, to make it lucid, and to grasp how it works, I propose that we seek to understand *how it unifies, brings together, or "synthesizes" two things that Tillich calls "dialectics" and "paradox."*

As noted in the introductory chapter of this book, this chapter and the next perform two distinct functions. They argue for the serious scholarly proposal I have just mentioned. But they also seek to make Tillich intelligible for those who know either nothing

---

[4]See 39n.3 in the next chapter.

about him or a lot about him. In order for this to work, I have
confined the inevitable scholarly debate to footnotes. Thus the
notes in this chapter and the next—or the long ones, in any case—
would probably be a distraction for readers who are just becoming
familiar with Tillich.

I have spoken of the "principal key" that I propose.[5] In order
for us to get a firm grip on it, however, I also provide in this
present chapter certain other "keys." I offer a ring of several keys,
as it were.

This chapter sets forth seven key passages in Tillich's writings
that are basic for what I want to show about his thought. Further,
the chapter also identifies a half-dozen or so concepts that are
stated in those basic texts. Since some of these concepts operate in
tandem, it makes sense to treat them as "concept pairs." Only in

---

[5]A word of caution is needed here. I am speaking in this chapter and the next
primarily of the "later" or "mature Tillich." This is the Tillich we meet especially,
though by no means only, in the three volumes of his *Systematic Theology* of
1951–1963. Sometime after about the mid-1940s, Tillich began using the term
"paradox" in a strict, technical sense. So far as I know, the earliest text in which
Tillich makes this sharp distinction is his "A Reinterpretation of the Doctrine of
the Incarnation," *Church Quarterly Review* (London) 147 (1949): 135-48; cf. 137,
equivalent to MW 6:306-16, cf. 308-309. In particular, the mature Tillich makes a
sharp distinction between "paradoxical" and "dialectical." By contrast, the earlier
Tillich treated the two ideas as more or less the same, as Marc Boss shows,
"*Coincidentia oppositorum*," 134-51, and as we can observe in Tillich's discussion
of "the religion of paradox" in a text originally published in 1925, namely, in Paul
Tillich, *What Is Religion*, ed. and trans. James Luther Adams (New York: Harper
& Row, 1969) 91-94. The point is obviously important for what I do in these two
chapters. If "paradox" and "dialectics" are roughly the same thing, a lot of the
excitement disappears from my claim that one of Tillich's great achievements was
to *synthesize* the two.

Marc Boss cites one text from the mature Tillich (which doubtless means
there are others) where the later Tillich uses the term "paradoxical" in his earlier,
broader sense. I take this to mean that, as with other people who adopt technical
terms, Tillich sometimes reverted and used the term in his earlier, broad sense.
His speaking in this way would pose a problem for my position only if Tillich
did it while dealing with his own theological ideas. In the text Boss cites,
however, Tillich is interpreting Kierkegaard. Boss cites Paul Tillich, *Perspectives
on 19th and 20th Century Protestant Theology*, ed. Carl E. Braaten (London: SCM
Press, 1967) 172-73. Boss, "*Coincidentia oppositorum*," 148-49.

the next chapter do I work out how these concepts and concept pairs figure in the larger body of Tillich's thought. However, I offer enough in this chapter to make them recognizable, and to give the reader a sense of where these concepts are leading us.

Finally, this chapter presents Tillich's understanding of two historical figures. I call them "historical archetypes" for his thought. More than any others, I believe, they make clear and concrete what I mean by my principal key, namely, the synthesizing of dialectics and paradox.

3. Historical Archetypes in Two Key Texts

Two historical figures have proved to be the inspiration for the two sides of Tillich's thought in which I am interested, that is, for "dialectics" and "paradox," respectively. The two are the Renaissance figure, Nicholas of Cusa (1401–1464), and the Reformation figure, Martin Luther (1483–1546), respectively. I should emphasize that I am not necessarily dealing here with the real historical Nicholas, or the real historical Luther. I am dealing with them *as Tillich understood them*. For my purposes, there are two important texts in which Tillich treats them together.

(1) The fuller of the two passages—which I am numbering as the first of my seven key texts—is a long passage from an important speech Tillich gave in 1959, "Dimensions, Levels, and the Unity of Life." The speech was a kind of "dress rehearsal" for the opening parts of the third and last volume of his *Systematic Theology*. Although neither "dialectics" nor "paradox" is explicitly mentioned in this passage, we shall see later that the concepts are here even if the terms are not.

> The protest against thinking in hierarchical levels was raised in the modern world both by Protestantism and the Renaissance. Luther, as well as Nicholas of Cusa, fought against the significance of the hierarchies in the vertical direction, the direction toward the ultimate. For Luther, there are no levels of proximity to God. Everyone stands on the level which was considered to be the lowest, that of the layman. The Saint is a sinner, and the sinner is just, not because he has climbed to the higher level, but because God's forgiveness has descended to him. The highest

degree of human perfection is still infinitely distant from the
infinite, just as the lowest degree. . . .

The same result has been reached in a religiously founded
humanism. Its classical representative is . . . Nicholas of Cusa. . . .
He meditates about the infinity of the infinite and realizes that
the infinite would cease to be the infinite if the finite stood beside
it as a limiting sphere. Therefore he established the principle of
the coincidence of opposites—the infinite in the finite and vice
versa. . . . This is the other way of undercutting the hierarchical
principle. It is the way that leads to modern humanism. (MW
6:403-405)

We might paraphrase Tillich's overall point in this passage by
saying that, according to Luther, all of us are equally far from God,
whereas, according to Nicholas, all of us are equally near.

Indeed, we are not only equally far and equally near; we are
infinitely far from God according to Luther, and *infinitely* near to
the divine according to Nicholas. Of course these "distances" are
not literal. They are qualitative rather than quantitative, and could
not be stated in meters, miles, or light years. Elsewhere Tillich
refers to Nicholas's kind of nearness as a "mystical" identity (ST
1:81). Or, in the language Tillich uses just above, Tillich says we
finite beings "coincide" with the infinite: the infinite is in us, as we
are also in the infinite.

In Luther's case, by contrast, we must be brought to God in a
surprising act of forgiveness. It is surprising because, though we
are sinners, we are accepted as just. When that happens we are, at
one and the same time, paradoxically both a godless sinner and a
justified person, that is, a person rightly related to God. Tillich
frequently emphasizes such paradoxes in his various writings.
When he does, the spirit of Luther is never far away. Often
enough, in such cases, Luther is either mentioned by name or his
famous phrase is quoted, *simul peccator et simul iustus* (or *simul
peccator, simul justus*), "at one and the same time sinner and
righteous" (ST 1:57; 2:92, 178).

Of interest here is Nicholas's reasoning—as Tillich represents
his reasoning. It is a quintessentially Tillichian way to argue. It
runs as follows. The finite cannot stand beside the infinite as a
limiting sphere: the infinite cannot be external to finite realities.
That would be self-contradictory, because in that case the finite

would be a *boundary* for the infinite: the infinite would "bump up against" the finite, and that would make the infinite finite, after all. Hence the finite and the infinite coincide. Each is within the other.

(2) The second of my featured texts is in large measure a condensed version of the first text. Nevertheless, it does add new elements in the second of its two sentences. The passage comes from the early part of volume 3 of Tillich's *Systematic Theology* (1963).

> It was not until Nicolaus Cusanus formulated the principle of the "coincidence of opposites" (for example, of the infinite and the finite) and Luther formulated the principle of "justification of the sinner" (calling the saint a sinner and the sinner a saint if accepted by God) that the hierarchical principle [the idea of ontological "levels" that prevailed in ancient and medieval times] lost its power and was replaced. Its place was taken in the religious realm by the doctrine of the priesthood of all believers and in the social-political realm by the democratic principle of equal human nature in every man. (ST 3:13)

4. Two Tendencies in a Tapestry

Tillich wishes to unite the contrasting tendencies we have just witnessed in Nicholas and Luther. And, as I have made clear, the principal key I propose for understanding him is that we see clearly and sharply the incredibly illuminating way in which his theology *combines* these two tendencies.

One of the two contrasting tendencies in Tillich's theology is "essentialist." It operates in terms of Tillich's "dialectic." The other tendency is "existentialist." It operates in terms of "paradox." I explain these terms fully in the next chapter, but we may think provisionally of the essentialist tendency as straightforwardly upbeat and optimistic, and we may think provisionally of the existentialist tendency as something that is downbeat, but with the surprising *reversal* of the pessimistic motifs that we have seen in Luther's idea of the paradox of justification.

The way we are related to the divine on the Nicholas side of Tillich's thought is dialectical, while the way we are related to God on the Luther side is paradoxical.

Tillich is persuaded that Nicholas's famous idea of "the coincidence of opposites" captures and also helps to foster the buoyant

spirit that many experience in the modern West. For Tillich this
coincidence of opposites refers especially to a coincidence of the
finite and the infinite, which includes the coincidence of the
human and the divine. Further—whether Nicholas himself conceived it precisely in this way or not[6]—Tillich construes this coincidence as a "dialectical identity of finite and infinite." Such an
"identity," as we shall see, is a lively kind of oneness that is full of
"Yes, we are the same," then "No, we are not the same," then Yes,
then No, and so on.

As Tillich sees it, it is in Luther that the ingredients for the
paradoxical side of Tillich's own thought appeared in history with
sufficient force to leave a mark on the modern era. In Luther's
thought, the chief example of this paradox is the way a person
who is justified by God's grace is simultaneously both ungodly
and righteous (Romans 4:5), a sinner far from God who is nevertheless simultaneously accepted through faith into intimate right
relation with God.

In the light of what we have just seen, I shall speak of Tillich's
theology not only as a synthesis of dialectics and paradox, but also
as a synthesis of Nicholas and Luther. This is a more concrete and
evocative way to speak, although it is a little less precise—at least
with regard to Nicholas.[7]

---

[6]Cf. Jasper Hopkins, *Nicholas of Cusa's Dialectical Mysticism* (Minneapolis:
Arthur J. Banning Press, 1988).

[7]Marc Boss is not convinced that Tillich takes Nicholas as a symbol or
historical archetype for the essentialist side of his thought. Boss points out that,
so far as he is aware, there is only one place where Tillich treats Nicholas as a
representative of essentialist ways of thinking (MW 1:414-16, a passage I shall
examine shortly), whereas there are several texts in which Tillich praises Nicholas,
along with a list of other figures, because they have an existentialist point of
view. Two of these texts come from the later Tillich, namely, ST 3:203, and Paul
Tillich, *The Courage to Be* (New Haven CT and London: Yale University Press,
1952) 131, cf. 130-32. Boss, "*Coincidentia oppositorum*," 138-39n.

On this particular issue I respond to Boss in two places. This note is the first
such place. In it I respond to the two passages just cited. Then in n. 11 of this
chapter, after presenting my own case, I shall be in position to complete the
response.

At the outset I acknowledge that Nicholas, though I believe Tillich features
him as the single best candidate for the job, is not so *clearly* archetypal for the

Tillich's thought is thus like a great tapestry in which we plainly see a seam running down the middle. The seam is the "synthesis" which I propose as the principal key to his theology. The fabric on one side of this seam is "essentialist" in Tillich's sense, a sense I explain further below (and see ST 2:23-24). It is also Renaissance Humanist in inspiration and in substance. The fabric on the other side of the seam is existentialist in Tillich's broad sense, also further explained below (and see ST 2:19-28). It is Protestant in inspiration and substance.

In saying that Nicholas of Cusa and Martin Luther serve as historical archetypes for Tillich's theological work, we are not engaging in a mere display of historical scholarship. The two individuals add concreteness and richness to what Tillich says on the subject of our interest. And their impact upon him is one of the reasons he wants to *say* those things.

---

dialectical-essentialist side of Tillich's thought as Luther is archetypal for the paradoxical-existentialist side. A great deal of Luther's work is summed up in "justification of the sinner through faith," and that Lutheran paradox constitutes, in turn, a great deal of the *paradoxical-existentialist side* of Tillich's thought. By contrast, the "overlap" is not so extensive between Nicholas and the *dialectical-essentialist side* of Tillich's theology. From Tillich's side, there are a lot of *non-Nicholas* elements in the dialectical-essentialist side of his thought, e.g., German idealist elements. And from Nicholas's side, the texts Boss cites tell us three things: that there are important *nonessentialist* elements in Nicholas in addition to the essentialist elements, that Tillich emphasizes and praises these existentialist elements, and that (at ST 3:203) Nicholas is listed with thirteen other figures in Western philosophy as "predominantly existentialist," though Tillich says it is "a matter of emphasis and not of exclusiveness."

However, the question at hand is not what Tillich praises in Nicholas (along with others) as an antecedent for his own existentialist point of view. The question rather is this: What does Tillich find in Nicholas (and only in him) that is new, that is formative for the entire modern era, and that Tillich explicitly tells us he appropriates as central to the dialectical-essentialist side of his own theology? I believe it will be clear from the seven texts I present in this chapter that the unique answer to that question is: Nicholas's idea of the coincidence of the finite and the infinite.

We may also note that Tillich says Hegel is "the classical essentialist" (ST 2:24), and yet also says that "the Existentialist elements in Hegel are much stronger than is usually recognized." Tillich, *The Courage to Be*, 134, found also at MW 5:203-204.

Nor is this just an individual or a personal matter. At least as Tillich understands the matter, these two figures have been most decisive in making two sets of ideas formative for the entire modern West. Thus, if Tillich's theology is adequately to connect with this modern situation, he must give an account of these ideas. And, of course, since Tillich belongs to the modern situation that these ideas have so heavily shaped, they are formative for him, also, as already noted.[8]

5. Why Not Hegel? A Third Key Passage

Nevertheless, so far as our two historical archetypes are concerned, the situation is a bit less clear-cut in the case of Nicholas than in the case of Luther. When Tillich wishes to refer to representatives of an essentialist outlook, he often appeals, not to Nicholas, but to classic German Idealism. And he calls Hegel "the classical essentialist" (ST 2:24).

Why not Hegel instead of Nicholas? When Tillich features Hegel in the way we have just observed, he usually has in mind the *excesses and exaggerations* of the essentialist side of life. Nicholas would be the example to follow, Hegel the extreme to avoid.

(3) This is precisely the way Tillich contrasted Nicholas with Hegel in a speech he gave in Japan in 1960, "Philosophical Background of my Theology." I number this passage as the third of my seven featured texts. In that place Tillich says his theology is an attempt to unite two lines in the history of philosophy since the time of Augustine, namely,

> the *essentialist line,* and the other which I will call the *existentialist line.* The one giving us the essences of being in empirical experience, and intuition; and the other which points to our human situation with its finitude, its foolishness, its ambiguities. (MW 1:416, cf. 414)

---

[8]Cf. Tillich's idea of "historical realism" in his "Realism and Faith" (MW 4:343-55), e.g., "Knowing the really real of our historical existence presupposes the knowledge of the really real in ourselves. . . . And knowing our historical situation on this level transforms our historical situation" (348), first published in Tillich, *The Protestant Era* (Chicago: University of Chicago, 1948) 73.

Tillich names four figures in the essentialist line, Augustine (who also appears in the existentialist line), Descartes, Nicholas, and Hegel. He picks out Nicholas to say that he is "a man who has influenced me especially" in that he

> expressed the principle of the coincidence . . . of the *infinite* and the *finite*. . . . The unity of the *infinite* and the *finite* has become one of the fundamental principles of my doctrine of religious experience. (MW 1:414)

Tillich then adds the caution that this essentialist line of thought

> has also its dangers. It can give man the feeling he sits, so to speak, in the center of the infinite itself. And this was the danger which came out most fully in . . . [German] classic philosophy. And here especially in Hegel. (MW 1:414-15)

Thus, as the best counterpart to Luther, we should recognize, not the nineteenth-century Hegel, but the fifteenth-century Nicholas of Cusa. Nicholas's thought (as Tillich appropriated it) is the historical archetype for the essentialist side of Tillich's thought more than is the case with any other single figure.

6. Concepts and Contrasts in Texts Four through Seven

In this section we turn to the final four passages in Tillich's writings that are basic for the case I make in this chapter and the next. In these texts Tillich gives brief and usually definitive explanations of about a half dozen concepts, or concept pairs. He also explains the contrasts he has in mind between the two sides of some of his concept pairs. In much of the next chapter I shall be unpacking these concepts and explaining these contrasts, as the headings for most of the sections in the next chapter make clear.

Here is a list of the concepts and contrasts that we shall encounter in the final four texts. I give them here, not in the order in which they are first mentioned in the passages, but in the order in which they will be explained in the next chapter:

- dialectics,
- the contrast between essence and existence (or between our essential being and our existence, and our "transition" from one of these two things to the other),

- the rational versus the irrational,
- the finite and the infinite (and the dialectical relation between them),
- estrangement (the irrational "gap" between our existence and our essential or potential being), and finally,
- paradox (and how it differs from what is "rational"; dialectics is rational).

(4) Our fourth text comes from the second volume of the *Systematic Theology* (1957):

> The paradox of the Christian message is not that essential humanity includes the union of God and man. This belongs to the dialectics of the infinite and the finite. (ST 2:94)

Here Tillich says (a) that the identity of the infinite and the finite is dialectical; (b) that, as human beings, one aspect of our essential (or created) being is our dialectical oneness with God; and (c) that there is a contrast between the dialectical and the paradoxical (or between the dialectical and the Christian paradox, in any case): the dialectical and the paradoxical are not the same.

(5) Our next text tells us something further about the dialectical unity of finite and infinite in Tillichian thought. It tells us once again that the dialectical and the paradoxical are different, but it also adds to that point the assertion that the dialectical is lively and dynamic. The passage is from 1949.

> Finiteness and infinity are correlated concepts; their unity is not paradoxical but, if I may use the abused term, dialectical, the one side driving necessarily to the other in mutual interdependence.[9]

(6) The sixth passage is one of Tillich's clearest statements that dialectical thinking is rational, while a "paradox" in Tillich's sense is *not* rational. I should quickly add something we shall see later, however. Though a paradox in this sense is not rational, it is not "irrational," either. Because this notion of paradox is central to our first two chapters and because a paradox is nonrational—it is neither rational nor irrational, but something in between—we shall

---

[9]Tillich, "A Reinterpretation of the Doctrine of the Incarnation," 137.

spend some time getting clear what Tillich means by "rational" in the next chapter.

> Dialectical thinking is rational, not paradoxical. . . . In a dialecti-
> cal description one element of a concept drives to another. . . .
> Trinitarian thinking is dialectical and in this sense rational, not
> paradoxical. This implies a relation in God between the infinite
> and the finite. (ST 2:90-91; cf. 1:56-57)

(7) Finally, in our seventh text we see Tillich bringing together, at least implicitly, all the concepts we have listed—the concepts we shall be unpacking in the next chapter. Before quoting the passage, some comments about its contents are in order.

Two of these contrasts appear for the first time in our texts, although we have mentioned them in our discussion, namely, (a) the contrast between "reason" and the "irrational," and (b) the difference between our "existence" and our "essence," which in this text also includes the idea that we (and all beings) make a transition from essence to existence when we actualize ourselves. Our essence or essential being is our God-given nature, including all the potentials that are built into us.

The term "infinite" does not explicitly appear in this seventh passage, but it is hard to miss the presence of the Nicholas-style dialectic of the finite and the infinite where Tillich speaks of "the finite manifestation of the divine Logos." The divine Logos of which he speaks is, of course, the second person of the Trinity. That means it is the divine Son who became incarnate in Jesus. But the Logos is more than that, as well. He (or She) is also the Son or divine Reason—Lady Wisdom in the Old Testament—through whom God the Creator brings the world into being as a rationally ordered whole (Proverbs 8; Wisdom 7–8; John 1; Colossians 1).[10]

Thus we come to the seventh key text itself. In the third volume of his system Tillich writes that

---

[10]Tillich's rendering of this biblical motif is spelled out in the next chapter in the heading entitled "Reason and the Rational World Built through Reason." The Ground of being, which is the first Trinitarian principle (the Father), brings the structured world into being *through* the second Trinitarian principle, the Logos.

the classical German philosophers . . . were right (and so were most classical theologians) in using the dialectics of life in order to describe the eternal process of the divine ground of being. The doctrine of the Trinity—this is our main contention—is neither irrational nor paradoxical but, rather, dialectical. Nothing divine is irrational—if irrational means contradicting reason—for reason is the finite manifestation of the divine Logos. Only the transition from essence to existence, the act of self-estrangement, is irrational. Nor is the doctrine of the trinity paradoxical. There is only one paradox in the relation between God and man, and that is the appearance of the eternal or essential unity of God and man under the conditions of their existential separation. . . . All other paradoxical statements in Christianity are variations and applications of this paradox, for example, the doctrine of justification by grace alone or the participation of God in the suffering of the universe (ST 3:284).[11]

---

[11]Having now made my case in the text that Nicholas is the historical archetype for the dialectical-essentialist side of Tillich's theology, I resume and conclude (from n. 7, above) my discussion of this specific issue with Marc Boss. Boss points out that, in at least two places (*The Courage to Be*, 130-32, and ST 1:86), Tillich praises the early Renaissance, including Nicholas, because it was theonomously aware of the *existential depth* of reason, whereas Tillich criticizes the later Renaissance because it was autonomously oriented only to the essentialistic *structure* of reason. This is further evidence, Boss thinks, that Tillich views Nicholas as an archetype for the existentialist side of his thought as much as, if not more than, for the essentialist side of his thought. Boss, "*Coincidentia oppositorum*," 138-39n.

To the contrary, Boss's further evidence seems to support my position. Precisely because the early Renaissance was relatively theonomous, the necessary conditions were not present for what Luther experienced. It was the oppressive heteronomy Luther suffered that made it possible—and desperately necessary!—for him to experience the justifying paradox with the sharp-edged, paradigmatic clarity that made it archetypal, as Tillich sees the matter, archetypal for the modern era and therewith also for Tillich. On the other hand, because of his existentialist point of view, Nicholas was able to give archetypically *existential* witness to what he experienced, namely, our relatively unestranged *essential* reality as finite humans who are dialectically identical with the infinite divine.

The Tillichian doctrine I state in condensed form in the preceding paragraph of this note is spelled out, in my understanding of it, in sects. 5 and 6 of the next chapter. One way to appreciate it is to say that the theonomous situation in which Nicholas lived was a bit like the kairos situation in which the early Tillich found

7. Conclusion

If the Nicholas-style, essentialist, and dialectical side of his thought were the whole story, Tillich would be a religious liberal. If the Lutheran, existentialist, and paradoxical side of his theology were all there was to it, Tillich would be a religious conservative. But Tillich is neither a liberal nor a conservative because he is a synthesis of both. That is one reason why he may be able to help us with the kinds of problems we talked about in the introduction of this book.

But if Tillich is to help us in this way, we must get into his thinking at a level of detail we have not yet managed to do.

---

himself. When this early Tillich gave existential witness to that kairos situation, his witness came out "essentialist," sometimes ecstatically so, because his existence (as he experienced it) was relatively unsplit from his essential, dialectical reality. That is the reason, as I say later, why the early Tillich did not carefully distinguish paradox from dialectics. Analogous things pertain in Nicholas's case.

Chapter 3

How Tillich's Theology Works: Synthesizing Dialectics and Paradox

We have seen in the preceding chapter that the major "join" in the entire edifice of Tillich's systematic theology—the "seam" that weaves together the two sides of the tapestry of his thought—is the fact that Tillich synthesizes dialectics and paradox, Nicholas of Cusa and Martin Luther. Using that insight as a key to his theological thinking, we are in a position to understand how his theology works.

I. Dialectics in Tillich

We begin with dialectics. Perhaps the easiest way to understand this Tillichian idea is to see how he contrasts dialectical knowledge with the kind of objective, "controlling knowledge" that we have in the natural and social sciences, and in their related technologies.

Tillich believes there is something shallow about such objectifying knowledge. It is detached and manipulative, and it mainly reflects what it knows from the outside. He thinks such knowledge fails to reach the depth of what it knows, and that it also fails to have any deep significance for the knower. By contrast, when we know things in a bit of depth, we grasp them in their essential being, and we ourselves are grasped in some measure by what these things are. That kind of knowledge is dialectical because it connects with life (MW 1:381-90).

Life, for Tillich, is the process in which beings actualize their potentialities. And every life process involves a triadic movement. First we beings integrate ourselves; secondly, we change, grow, and reach beyond ourselves; and thirdly, we return back into ourselves—although these three moves are going on simultaneously in a process of gradual change, movement, or development (ST 3:30-32).

In a more dramatic fashion, Tillich often speaks of his dialectic in twofold terms. He can do this because we are bipolar beings and, like all living things, we are constantly going beyond ourselves and returning to ourselves (ST 1:56, 234; 2:90-91; 3:31-32; MW 6:403-407). Yet, so long as we exist at all, these two opposed moves do not fall apart. Nor do they pull us apart. And the reason they do not split us apart is that, when we actualize our bipolar nature, a third element enters the picture. This third element is the *unity* of the two opposed moves.

This unity is not static, and it is not something achieved, once and for all. As we move through time, we try always to keep our two counterposed tendencies together, unified. And we *succeed* in doing that—more or less. We are forever seeking and we are forever finding *fresh new syntheses* of the opposed tendencies that make up our essential being.

But notice how easily problems can break out at this point. What if we do not fully unify the two opposite poles of our reality? And, of course, we never do. Not fully. We never manage to actualize all our polar possibilities in a *full* way, a fully *balanced* way, and a *creative* way.

This will become much clearer if we look at an example. One of the bipolar possibilities built into our essential reality is the way we are able both (a) to be "our own person" and (b) to participate intimately in the lives of others. Ideally we do both of these things fully and well because we are essentially bipolar. But the actual is never up to the ideal. It is difficult to get the balance right. And when things begin to go awry, nasty and destructive consequences often follow.

Perhaps we strike out on our own in such a separate and individualized way that we never listen, we never connect deeply with others. Or, by contrast we merge ourselves so thoroughly into a family, a relationship, or a circle of friends that we hardly think of ourselves, we fail to think *for* ourselves, and we never get around to living our own dream. Or, in a third case, we may veer first in one of these two directions and then in the other.

Tillich calls this particular situation the conflict between "individualization and participation." In our essential or potential reality we are both fully individualized and fully participant in the lives of others. But in the process of actualizing our potential, our existence turns out to be only a poor approximation of our God-given essence. In many respects, our life is a *contradiction* of the bipolar persons that we essentially are. And this tension between individuality and participation is only one in a list of conflicts that Tillich analyzes (ST 1:174-78, cf. 163-210).

One reason it is a serious matter when we fall into contradiction with our essential being is that, in our bipolar reality, we are not only essentially related to other people. We are also essentially one with God. "If we love one another, God lives in us" (1 John 4:12). Thus, when our actual living contradicts our essential bipolar reality, our lives contradict our oneness with God. "Those who say, 'I love God,' and hate their brothers or sisters, are liars" (1 John 4:20 NRSV).

2. Two Trajectories: Essence and Existence

At this point it will help if I bring a graph into the discussion. The graph has two axes, a horizontal axis and a vertical axis. Two arrows, gently curved and mostly parallel, streak across this graph from left to right. This represents movement through time, because the horizontal axis is a "time" axis. The arrows' movement from left to right describes the course of creaturely life *through time*.

By contrast, the vertical axis is a "better vs. worse" axis. The higher arrow is *more developed* or *better* or *more fulfilled*, while the lower arrow is less of each of those things, or it can mean *worse*, and sometimes *destructive* if not downright *evil*.

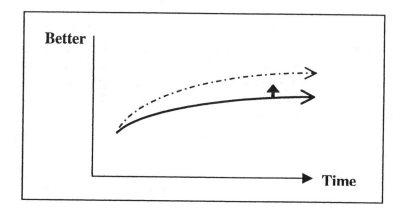

More specifically, the upper arrow represents our accumulating human *potentialities*, that is, what our life as individuals and as a human race *could be*; the lower arrow represents our actual lives, that is, the way our personal and collective lives on this planet are *actually turning out*—from moment to moment, from year to year, and from century to century. In summary, the upper line is essence. It is our essential being, our vast and always-growing potential. The lower line is existence. It is the way our lives are actualized from one existential situation to the next.

The two arrows are joined at the left. They begin their trajectory through time together. But the lines quickly diverge. A gap appears between them. I leave the lower arrow for later comment. The upper line is the historical trajectory in which more and more of our enormous human potentialities are being actualized (or *could* be actualized). It is a constant crescendo of human affairs at their best.

This is a dialectical process in the sense explained in the previous section. That means it is full of tension. That tension is exciting and promising; but it is also dangerous and potentially lethal. Further, the upper line is also fully meaningful—or fully "rational," a term I explain in the next section.

There was at least one period of Tillich's life in which he experienced a lot of the good things I have just described. In the events that took place in Germany from 1918 into the early 1920s, he sensed the meaningfulness and rationality of the situation in an intense way. In the explosion of culture that marked the early years of Weimar Germany—in emerging styles in the arts, new governmental forms, evolving social practices, and advances in the sciences—Tillich experienced something he called a "kairos," or a "fullness of time." Or better, he sensed it as a *relative* fullness. He was under no illusion that the Kingdom of God had completely arrived.[1]

---

[1]For example, see Tillich's, "On the Idea of a Theology of Culture" (1919), now in his *What Is Religion?* ed. James Luther Adams (New York: Harper, 1969), original German in MW 2:69-86; and Tillich, *The Religions Situation* (New York: Meridian Books, 1956), a translation by H. Richard Niebuhr that was first published in 1932 of Tillich, *Die religiöse Lage der Gegenwart* (1926), MW 5:27-98.

What of the lower of my two trajectories? From time to time we may sense that things don't add up. The world is out of joint. Things have lost their reason. Politics is a fraud, the schools are a madhouse, the family has collapsed, the country is going down the drain, religion only makes people smug, our own life is a blind alley, and there is absolutely nothing new under the sun. Everything is pointless, utterly pointless (Ecclesiastes 1 and 8–9).

To be sure, when people have such feelings in a severe way, they may be ill. If so, they need expert help or treatment. But, as the biblical Book of Ecclesiastes reminds us, perfectly normal people are sometimes touched by feelings of this kind, sometimes quite strongly. To whatever extent these people are normal and their perceptions are rational, to that extent the state of their culture and their society is irrational—according to the larger sense of "reason" that Tillich uses.

3. Reason and the Rational World Built through Reason

Our upper arrow, as we have said, is a picture of the stupendous attainments of the many cultures that have flourished, and are now flourishing, on this planet. We can itemize: the upper arrow is (a) the knowledge that is gained in the inquiries of these cultures; (b) the expressiveness that is manifest in their art; (c) the justice and welfare that are achieved in their statecraft, economy, and technology; and (d) the love and "belongingness" that are experienced in their communities.

The four spheres I have just listed—the *cognitive*, the *esthetic*, the *organizational* (or technical-political-legal), and the *organic* (or communal-social)—are four "fields" of ontological reason (ST 1:77).[2] More precisely, they are four fields of "objective reason." As the previous paragraph shows, these fields are four spheres that we recognize in our *objective world*, that is, the world of human affairs that engages us because it makes livable sense—or is "rational."

---

[2]I have incorporated into the fields of reason the technical act that Tillich does not formally discuss until his analysis of culture in ST 3:57-62. But, as I concluded in my dissertation, "the functions of culture may be discussed as functions or reason, or vice versa." James, "Symbolic Knowledge of God," 139.

Corresponding to this objective reason is "subjective reason." Whereas objective reason is "out there" giving intelligible structure to the world, subjective reason is "in us" and in our actions. Subjective reason is the way in which we, as perceiving subjects, "grasp" reality; and subjective reason is also the way we, as acting persons, outwardly "shape" reality. (The two terms in quotation marks are Tillich's chosen terms for the two "functions" of subjective reason.)

To explain: In *grasping reality*, we and all beings "receive" it. As we grasp it, reality enters us, unites with us, and we share its powers. In *shaping reality*, we and all beings "react." We shape, reshape, and leave our mark upon the objective world. When we shape the world, and even when we grasp it, we help to make it what it is, namely, a meaningful place in which we can "have a life," as we might say today (ST 1:75-79).

It is not too much to say that, for Tillich, *we construct the world*, the objective world that can be rationally grasped. When we say that, however, it is important quickly to say three other things. (1) The "we" who construct the world are not just human beings. We the builders of the world are *all beings*, from atoms and molecules to mountains and stars, with all the entities in between, organic and inorganic (MW 402-16).

(2) The overwhelming majority of the construction that produces our world has been done in our past. To speak only of one species of beings, we marvel at the legacy our human forebears have left us. From their grasping and shaping of their world, they have left us the languages we speak, the institutions that give order to our lives, the technologies that multiply our powers, and much more. We do not make the world from scratch.

(3) Finally, the infinite Creator has made the world, and is forever remaking it and sustaining it. But that most certainly does not exclude the roles we finite beings play. Infinite creative power does all this *through* the countless finite beings. As Nicholas of Cusa said, the infinite is within the finite and "coincides" with it; and as Tillich understands this (see section 3 of the previous chapter), infinite creativity coincides with our creativity in a lively dialectic in which we almost hear a dialogue: "We two are the same. No we aren't. Yes. No. . . . " and so on. The infinite no

sooner affirms itself through something we do than the infinite goes *beyond* that achievement (that is the "No" we hear) in order to call for something more, fuller, greater (that is the "Yes" again).

When we look at this construction job both over the long haul and "right now," we see that the world is being constantly hammered into shape—into the shape it takes in each new instant—by a billion trillion hammer blows per nanosecond. Or, dropping the hammer metaphor, our world at each successive instant is the accumulated result of the countless ways in which we, and an infinity of other beings, have grasped and shaped reality, from moment to moment, from month to month, from age to age.

This does not mean our world is a dream that we can dream any way we wish. Our biological environment dwarfs us, and our physical environment outsizes us a trillionfold to the billionth power. And these twin environments are stubbornly "there." They bend very little to our will. The reason they bend so little is that a colossal number of animal, vegetable, mineral, and other inorganic beings have for a *very* long time been in the business—and they are *still* in the business—of hammering and shaping our surroundings into the starry expanse we see, the earth, water, and wind we touch, and the myriad creatures of forest, land, and sea that we know and know about.

Only when that gargantuan work is done can our race appear. But once we are here, our role in creating "our world" is vast. The Bible is aware of this. With its extremely realistic notion of what a "name" is, Genesis tells us that "whatever the man called every living creature, *that was its name*" (Genesis 2:19 NRSV, emphasis added).

As soon as we human beings appear within our environment on this planet, our creative role begins. It begins with the question, What shall we make of it? What shall we "make of it" as we perceive it and construe it? What shall we make of it, literally, in our outward shaping? And the thing we are always making out of our environment is a world, that is, the rationally meaningful world of human projects and affairs.

We can conclude this account of our world making by showing how Tillich matches up the two subjective functions of reason with its four objective fields. The theme or plot of this matchup is the fact that we carry out our subjective and individual activities *according to* principles and factors that belong to objective reason.

We begin with our grasping or perceiving, which we do both in a cognitive and in an esthetic way, as we have seen. We find out what we know (a) *according to* objective principles of evidence and truth, and we appreciate things esthetically (b) *according to* what is "objectively" or intersubjectively good in the broad sense of "good art." We do our active, outward shaping of the world according to the remaining two fields of objective reason. As we shape and reshape the organized world of human affairs, we act (c) *according to* rational principles of what gets the job done, and what justly gives all parties their due. And when we participate in the life and growth of families, friendships, communities, and societies, we are guided (d) *according to* rational principles of "love," that is, according to the way kinship groups are formed, societies bond, and caring relationships evolve.

In these four ways—and in a thousand mixtures of these ways—the meaningful world we occupy comes into being. And it happens that way because subjective reason in us grasps and shapes *according to* the objective reason that gives structure to the world and lets it make sense.

4. The Gap between Essence and Existence: Bad News, Good News

The lovely picture I have just drawn is not totally false. If it were absolutely false, nothing could exist, or nothing that we could possibly know, in any case. There would be no order or structure, no rhyme or reason, in *anything*. There would be no world. Only chaos.

But, if our lovely picture of a rational world is not sheer falsehood, it is also not the whole truth, either. We may hark back to our diagram. As the lower arrow there is trying to tell us, we grasp our world *more or less* according to what is true and meaningful; and we shape that world *more or less* according to what is right and wholesome. Or, stating this in an inverse way, our world is always more or less *irrational*. Sometimes more, sometimes less, our world is an irrational mess because we human beings are always making an irrational mess of it. Granted, some of our "falling short" is due to our finite limits, our being subject to honest error. But there is something much more sinister at work too, something the Bible calls "sin."

That is the reason for one of the features of the diagram that I have yet to comment upon. The upper arrow must be drawn with a dotted line. Why not a solid line? The reason is that the upper arrow is not factual. It is a grand narrative written *in the subjunctive mood*. That dotted line traces what our historical human life *were*—subjunctive "were"—*if* we were always in the process of *fully* and *undistortedly* actualizing our essential possibilities, including our potential for living rationally.

By contrast, the lower arrow is drawn with a solid line because it is a story told in the *indicative* mood. It is the human story as we have actually written it—and as we keep on writing it—in hate, in destruction, and in the heartache of a thousand shattered dreams.

To be sure, the story we have written includes many beautiful and inspiring things. But the uplifting side of the human enterprise is not my focus for the moment. My present interest is the *gap* between the two lines. The gap between these two trajectories is the distance between what we could be and what we are. It is the measure of how far short we fall. It is, in fact, *the* Fall, the Adamic Fall (ST 2:55-59).

This gap makes graphic what Tillich means when he says we "exist." To exist, he says, is to "stand out of" our potential or essential being. Looked at in one way, my graph turns certain things upside down. To compensate, we need to imagine that we "stand downward." While our essential or potential being is on the upper arrow, our existence—the way we actually live—"stands out of" that. It "stands out" *downward* because our existence is located on the lower line.

This is not to gainsay the fact that we finite creatures actualize some stunning possibilities, individually and collectively. Those achievements are the forward and upward movement on my diagram. But in every such advance, we also confirm our fallenness. At each successive moment we *reposition ourselves* in a number of ways at a lower point on the vertical axis. Although the gap between the lines narrows in some times and places, my main point stands. Whether the gap is wide or narrow, it is always there. And it always hurts.

Despite all this, there are two pieces of good news along with all the bad.

(1) The first piece of good news is that the gap between the arrows never involves a total separation between the two lines. Our existence can never be totally divorced from our essence, Tillich believes. In that respect, the graph could be misleading, because it shows two lines that are completely separate, once they part ways at the beginning.

In this connection we might advert once more to Tillich's metaphor of "standing out." "An actual thing stands out of mere potentiality," he says, "but it also remains in it" (ST 2:21). To exist is a little like standing knee-deep in water. In existing, we stand out of our potential being—although we continue also to stand in it. We continue forever to participate in our life-giving, essential being even while we are at a distance and estranged from it.

Or, to put this another way, what we essentially are is always *in* us, and we are in it, because it is what we *are*, in essence. That— our essential or our potential being—is what God is constantly creating and sustaining us to be (ST 1:254-58). Apart from that ontological backbone, we would melt into sheer nothingness, or never rise from the void.

(2) The second piece of good news is the news that most interests me at this point. It is *the* good news. In the form in which the Christian community experiences it, this news is the Gospel that God graciously closes the gap in "Jesus as the Christ," that is, in Jesus received as the one though whom the age of salvation comes (ST 2:118-38, 165-70).

God does this directly from out of the transcendent. "In Christ *God* was reconciling the world to himself" (2 Corinthians 5:19, emphasis added). This healing event happens on the vertical axis in an upward move that takes hold of our two arrows and *brings them back together.*

We may represent this reconciling, healing, saving action by a vertical-upright arrow between the two lines—a single arrow, although the reconciling action is actually taking place along much of the length of the horizontal lines.

What does it mean to say this reconciling move is vertical, and not an action on the horizontal axis? It means that the reconciliation is not a matter of our finite endeavors or accomplishments. Our restored oneness with the divine is not something we can ever make happen purely on our own. We cannot force it or grab it. We can fake it and claim to have it. We often do. But we do not deserve it. And we can never *possess* it. It comes purely as a gift.

5. The Reconciling Act: Symbolic and Nonrational

How are we to understand the vertical act of reconciliation that we have just presented, the "upright arrow" as I have represented it? How are we to understand it not just graphically, but also conceptually? Three things need to be said about it. I say two of those things in this section, and the third in the next. Here I explain what it means to say this reconciling act is symbolic, and what it means to say it is nonrational. In the next section, we shall see that these first two statements have carried us some distance toward understanding the third thing we need to say, namely, that the reconciling act is paradoxical.[3]

---

[3]At this point I am far enough along in making my case that I can explain what I meant when I said, in the introduction to the previous chapter, that the idea of "synthesizing dialectics and paradox" helps to make Tillich's method of correlation "more intelligible," and to "explain" it.

What theology does, according to "correlation," is to correlate the main existential questions in a given situation with the religious symbols that are alive in that situation. But "correlation" is a clumsy and imprecise notion (see its three meanings, ST 1:60-61). It becomes more intelligible when we say that, when theology "correlates," it clarifies (or *should* clarify) what is happening where the point of the vertical-upright arrow approaches the higher horizontal arrow and achieves an intersection, or near intersection, with it. At that almost intersection, the reconciling action of the infinite is lifting our lower-line existence and reuniting us (more fully) with our own depth and, more generally, reuniting us (more fully) with all of our higher-line possibilities.

The epistemic relations involved come into focus when we show—as I am about to show in my text—that the reconciling action that grasps us and brings us closer to such an intersection is (1) symbolic, (2) nonrational (i.e., it is more than, and other than, merely rational), and (3) paradoxical. All this is in Tillich's "correlation," but it is obscured when the question-answer arrangement splits so widely asunder a number of details that need to be seen together—if we are to

(1) First as to symbol. The reconciling action from out of the transcendent certainly grasps us. But speaking in purely this-worldly, literal terms, this saving action is not "there." That is, it is not there simply as one more literal fact within the objective world of space and time that we have a part in making. It is too large a thing for that. It is too "enveloping" an event to be contained within the world that *we finite beings* grasp, shape, and help create.

On the other hand, if the restorative action of the infinite is to get at us where we live, it must do so *through* some of the objects, persons, and events within our world. Thus the situation is two-sided. We cannot grasp the transcendent. It must grasp us. But it must do so through things we can grasp, that is, through things within our world.

That gives us a workable definition of the religious symbol in Tillich's sense (MW 253-78, 415-20). Religious symbols are those persons, things, and events within our world through which we are "gotten at" by the saving, reconciling action that I have plotted as the vertical-upright arrow on my diagram. Thus, if something is a symbol, it is full of a great deal "more" than what it is. For example, the Christian message is transformingly powerful even beyond what it literally says, if and insofar as it is symbolic in Tillich's strong sense—if and insofar as it is the vehicle of this "more." And the same is true of any really life-transforming gospel.

(2) Now for our second statement about the reconciling act. If we say it is not rational in Tillich's sense, we mean that the "more" that is in the symbol enters into our rational existence from *beyond reason*. It comes as an eruption out of what Tillich calls "the depth

---

understand them.

I can only hint at how my proposal helps not merely to make correlation intelligible, but also to "explain" it. By connecting Tillich's early-and-late concept of "dialectics" with his later concept, "paradox," we see how Tillich's intensified experience of "the gap" (from the 1930s into the 1950s) drove him from a triadic theological method (MW 2:70-72; GW 1:222-26, 300-301) to the two-part method of correlation—although the triadic method underlies the later method, telling its component parts "what they should do." See James, "Symbolic Knowledge of God," 247-54.

of reason." And this depth is something that is not reason, but "precedes" reason (ST 1:80).

This explains something the reader may not have noticed in section 3 above. As I tried to show how various cultures are meaningful, I several times presented the four fields of reason. These fields give structure, meaning, and sense to the cultures, I said. But I never acknowledged that each of these cultures also had a religious sector—although of course each of them does.

Why the omission? In part I was waiting until now to consider the religious symbol. But the main reason I left religion off those cultural maps is that I was discussing reason and, for Tillich, organized religion is not one of the proper fields or functions of reason. In fact, there is an interesting sense in which a special religious sphere should not even exist. To quote Tillich:

> There should be neither myth nor cult ["religion" in the usual sense]. They contradict essential reason; they betray by their very existence the "fallen" state of reason which has lost immediate unity with its own depth. It has become "superficial," cutting itself off from its ground and abyss.[4]

Tillich's point is that everything we do and say and achieve and enjoy *should* be so full of the presence of the divine that we do not need special religious organizations or activities to experience that presence and to "live that presence," every moment of every day. In such a situation, "going to church" would be totally redundant. Everywhere would *be* church—everywhere and nowhere—because no special place would have to serve that function. It would be like heaven. In heaven there is no temple because *God* is the temple (Revelation 21:22).

As Tillich explains this, reason is essentially "transparent toward its depth in each of its acts and processes," but "in

---

[4]ST 1:80. When Tillich says here that religion's symbolic discourse and activity "contradict essential reason," he does not mean they are "irrational." To the contrary, as we have seen, their function is partially to *reverse* the irrationality that infects our existence. He means—as I quote him two paragraphs later in my text —that religions, by standing alongside the proper functions and fields of reason as something separate, or as something that does not fit within them, belie the fact that reason in its own functions is *essentially united* with its own depth.

existence this transparency is opaque and is replaced by" religious symbolisms (ST 1:80). If our lives were all they could be and should be—if the earth were "full of the knowledge of the LORD as the waters cover the sea" (Isaiah 11:9)—we would not need religious symbols. The "more" that is imported into our existential situation by religious symbols would not need to be imported. It would already be there.

Let us look closely at how, in such a fulfilled situation, the "more" that the religious symbol imports into our existence would already be "there." Let us see how this "more" would already be effective in each of the fields and functions of reason. Each time we knew any given thing, we would find it translucent to the truth of all that is. Each time we appreciated the expressiveness of some story, song, or image, we would find it charged with the beauty that suffuses and makes wonderful everything that we perceive. In each aspect of our larger life with others there would be something so very "right" about our practices and our institutions that they would declare the majesty of justice itself. And in each caring relationship, in every gesture of affection, we would feel ourselves claimed and sustained by the depthless love that never lets us go (ST 1:80).

But obviously our situation does not have the "more" I have tried to illustrate in the preceding paragraph. This "more" is for the most part "squeezed out of" our seeing and our doing. Therefore, if this "more" is to assert itself and be experienced at all, it must set up a special sphere within our cultures, namely, religion! And it must "get at us" through special religious events, special things, special people, or special places, namely, through religious symbols. We might state Tillich's point thus: Since church isn't everywhere, we have to go to church!

6. Tillich's New Category of "Paradox"

I can think of a mischievous sense in which, during the years when Tillich's systematic thought was evolving, he almost painted himself into a corner. On the one hand, he is stoutly opposed to any suggestion that the symbolism of the Christian message should be categorized as absurd, illogical, or irrational. Quite to the contrary, it is immensely meaningful (ST 1:56-57; 2:90-92; 3:284).

And the same applies for any truly reconciling gospel. Yet, as we saw in the last section, it is also important to Tillich to say that the good news of religion does not fit the category of "the rational," either. If it is not rational and not irrational either, what is it?

At this point Tillich opens an unexpected door and escapes from the corner into which he had almost painted himself. He comes up with a new category. The motion *downward* on my vertical axis is irrational (ST 2:91). It is the Fall, the irrational transition from essence to existence. But for the restorative action upward that *reverses* some of the downward move of the Fall, Tillich adopts a new category, the category of "paradox" (ST 1:56-57; 2:90-92).[5]

How does Tillich explain this new category—"new" since sometime around 1940–1945? He exploits the etymology of the term "paradox" in order to stamp the term with his own definition. He points out that the word literally means "against the opinion." The symbols that make up the Christian message are "against the opinion" in the following sense. Their import is contrary to the oppressive climate of opinion that prevails *in our estranged existence.*

Thus the meaningfulness of the saving symbol is not a contradiction of reason itself. It is a contradiction of those ugly and *irrational* facts—the meanness, brokenness, pointlessness, and nagging guilt—that we suffer and often take for granted with a sigh (ST 1:56-57; 2:92).

Even when we are grasped by the power of the good news, many of these ugly facts remain. However, we are reunited with the Ground and Aim of our existence *despite all that.* In terms of our graph, we are accepted from out of the transcendent, or on the vertical axis, even though, when we look at ourselves on the horizontal line and observe where that line is located, we see how unacceptable we are. This thesis—the thesis that we are accepted

---

[5]ST 1:56-57; 2:90-92. In my dissertation I map out what I call "the episte-mological matrix of the religious symbol." Among the conclusions reached in that analysis is the one just stated, namely, that the religious symbol is not dialectical-rational, it is not reflectively rational and, indeed, it is not properly rational at all (though it is not irrational, either, as we have seen). Rather, the epistemological status of the saving religious symbol is "paradox." See James, "Symbolic Knowledge of God," 187-210.

despite our being unacceptable—is one of the things Tillich is most famous for stating.[6] The thesis is practically a definition of "paradox." Our being reconciled with God is contrary to and against all the commonsense, taken-for-granted assumptions and expectations of the world in which we live.

Though I am dealing primarily with the mature Tillich in this and the preceding chapter, I can strengthen my case by harking back to what we said in section 2 above about Tillich during his early years after the First World War. Because this early Tillich experienced a kairos or a fullness of time, he felt little of the gap between my two arrows. It was as though the two lines on my graph *had almost completely converged*—as though the upright arrow of the kairos had brought them virtually together.

In the complete kairos of the Kingdom of God—which is our ultimate destiny, the goal of history—the lines of the two arrows *will* totally converge. Paradox and dialectics will coincide. Or rather, paradox will disappear. The glad, rational, dialectical unfolding of events will be the whole truth about what is going on. There will be no "discouraging word"—no engrained, fallen, "sick" opinion that the good news of God's nearness *needs* to reverse and contradict in a "paradoxical" way.

Since the young Tillich felt that he had experienced a foretaste of this kind of healed and fulfilled life around 1920, it is not surprising that he had not yet felt the need to distinguish sharply between the two terms, paradox and dialectics, though he would do so later.[7]

---

[6]Paul Tillich, "You Are Accepted," in Paul Tillich, *The Shaking of the Foundations* (New York: Charles Scribner's Sons, 1948) 153-63.

[7]Responding to Marc Boss in n. 5 of the preceding chapter, I opined that the later Tillich, despite an occasional use of "paradox" in his old, loose sense, continued to stand by his new distinction between paradox and dialectics—certainly so when his own thought was at stake. However, Boss cites two further texts *from the later Tillich*, both quoted below, that might seem to militate against my position. In these texts Boss makes it reasonably clear he thinks Tillich is saying the following. The principles that Nicholas and Luther advocate, coincidence of opposites and justification, are one principle. Boss, "*Coincidentia oppositorum*," 140-42.

I am not convinced that Tillich is discussing justification in these texts, though he is discussing Luther. As I read them, these texts show that Tillich found in Luther not only the soteriological paradox (which I think Tillich featured as Luther's major contribution to the shaping of the modern West), but that Tillich also found in Luther what I would call a certain philosophicotheological principle, one that has to do with creation or providence rather than with salvation, namely, the Nicholas of Cusa-like coincidence of opposites, a coincidence that I think Tillich formulates as the dialectical coincidence of finite and infinite, human and divine.

Now the two texts. (1) The first is Tillich, *Perspectives on 19th and 20th Century Protestant Theology*, [transcribed and] edited by Carl E. Braaten (New York: Harper & Row, 1967) 77, 78. Some explanation is necessary because Marc Boss used the German version: Tillich, *Ergänzungs- und Nachlassbände zu den Gesammelte Werke*, vol. 2, ed. Renate Albrecht (Stuttgart: Evangelisches Verlagswerk, 1972) 62. The work of Tillich's here cited was originally a tape (not available to me) of lectures Tillich gave in English in 1963. When Renate Albrecht translated them, she also listened to the tapes afresh. In a late-March or early-April 2002 telephone conversation, Braaten advised me that Albrecht was occasionally more confident than he of what Tillich was saying on the tape. Thus she translated into her German verson some things Braaten had not included.

In this first of my two texts Tillich says, "Luther in his discussions of the presence of the divine in the sacramental materials of bread and wine used similar formultions" to those of Nicholas; and Tillich paraphrases Luther: "God is nearer to everything than anything is to itself. He is fully in every grain of sand, but the whole world cannot comprehend him" (*Perspectives*, 77). Then Tillich concludes (in my back-translation of something in Albrecht's German that is not fully included in Braaten's English transcription): "Thus mysticism, Luther, and Nicholas have a common basis out of which the principles of the modern philosophical and theological understanding of God and the world have developed, and upon which the modern mind grounds its ultimate concern."

(2) In Tillich, "Reinhold Niebuhr's Doctrine of Knowledge," in *Reinhold Niebuhr: His Religious, Social, and Political Thought*, ed. C. W. Kegley and R. W. Bretall (New York: Macmillan, 1956) 38-39, Tillich says, "the elements of ancient dualism which crept into Christian thought, and which were never completely removed, not even in the Reformation, have prevented Niebuhr from accepting the principle of the 'coincidence of the opposites' which is expressed both in the philosophy of the Renaissance (Nicholas Cusanus) and in the theology of the Reformers (Luther)."

From these texts and my discussions with Boss I have gained the "enriched idea of paradox" that I mention in n. 1 of the previous chapter. It goes as follows. The Tillichian Luther views justification as the repair of a breach. But a breach presupposes a prior unity that it restores. Given the undoubted Lutheran principle that "the finite is capable of the infinite," it is clear (in Tillich's Luther) that Luther understands this prior unity as a Nicholas-type coincidence of finite and infinite. Thus, despite the sharp difference between paradox and dialectics in the

7. The Renaissance: Necessary, But Not Enough

If we have received good news of such significance that its power transcends reason itself, do we still need the Renaissance? Should we ignore Nicholas, forget about the infinite possibilities of the human race and, like the aged prophet Anna, stay in the temple night and day, worshiping God with prayer and fasting (Luke 2:37)?

By no means. The paradoxical closing of the gap is not a contradiction of reason. It is the healing of reason, or the partial healing of reason, in any case. It is the restoration, in beginning and power, of the essential reasonableness of our lives. Hence we can say—the sentiment is Tillich's if the statement is not—that we would no more wish to miss the Renaissance than we would wish to miss puberty.

In both cases, however, there is some temptation. In the case of the Renaissance, the danger is the effort at self-salvation. Since the infinite is in us, we think we own it. We believe we shall reach the stars, figuratively speaking. Almost inevitably we try to make for ourselves a name above every name.

But down that road there is no salvation. Down that road lurks only the emptiness of a soon-exhausted, self-sufficient finitude.[8] Or worse, down that road lies fanaticism and the murderous clash of finite absolutes, each demonically laying waste to the other (ST 3:102-106).

Whence cometh our help, then? Here comes Luther now, bringing the Gospel! And he is bringing it in the wheelbarrow of paradox. To paraphrase St. Paul, it is not in the lofty words of wisdom, and not in reason, human or divine, but rather in the foolishness of the Gospel that the healing answer comes (1 Corinthians 1:21). Grace grasps us vertically from beyond through the symbol, the lowly symbol, as paradox.

---

mature Tillich, the Lutheran paradox (in the later Tillich's view) *presupposes* the dialectical identity of finite and infinite; and in that sense dialectics is *partly constitutive* of paradox. Paradox is the negation of a negation. It is the restorative or salvific negation of the existential negation of dialectics.

[8]Tillich's phrase is "in sich ruhende Endlichkeit," MW 5:91, 96, and 27-97 passim.

8. Conclusion

It has been our purpose in this chapter to understand how Tillich's theology works in order that we might use that theology as we deal with our encounters with other faiths.

What have we learned? If am correct, we have put our finger on the main "joint" in the systematic structure of Tillich's theology; and, in so doing, we have learned how his theology works. Along the length of the "seam" I have described, Tillich is constantly sewing together the two panels of a monumental tapestry. In that seam he achieves a stunning synthesis of dialectics and paradox, Nicholas and Luther, essence and existence, liberal and conservative.

How can that help us? Having seen how Tillich does it, we may be able to do it, too—if we wish. We may find ourselves able to bring together (1) the *broad and generous instincts* of liberals, who see the glint of the infinite in all things, even in other religions (that is our "Nicholas-dialectics" theme), and (2) the *intensity and down-to-earthness* of conservatives, who know how very much they depend upon the truth and power that grasp them in their own particular faith (that is our "Luther-paradox" theme).

What exactly would it mean to hold those two things together? How precisely might we go about it? And is that really what we want to do? Those questions—along with a range of related questions—will concern us as we proceed.

PART TWO

Finding the Best Attitudes in Interreligious Encounters

Chapter 4

Rethinking the Typology of Pluralism, Inclusivism, and Exclusivism

In the introduction to this book, we looked briefly at the tripartite typology that has become familiar since the 1980s. According to that typology, people have just one of three attitudes toward religions other than their own. Their attitude will be *exclusivist* if they believe that saving or ultimately fulfilling truth is to be found exclusively in their own religion. Their attitude will be *pluralistic* if they believe that each of the great world religions is an equally valid and equally effective vehicle of truth and salvation. And their attitude will be *inclusivist* if they believe that religious truth and salvation are normatively given in their own faith, although other traditions include more or less of that truth and salvation.

Tillich never had occasion to deal with this typology. He died in 1965. Had he dealt with it, I think he would have found the typology deficient, but potentially useful. In this chapter, I use Tillich's ideas to rethink the typology and to reconstruct it so it can be useful today. The main Tillichian doctrine I employ is Tillich's view that our experience takes place at three different depths or levels. There is a first level that is theoretical and detached, a second level at which we experience empathy, insight, and understanding, and a third depth at which we are profoundly, existentially, and life-shapingly involved with what we are encountering.

Although our "insider" involvement in a religion is basically a level-three, existential kind of thing, we can relate to our own faith at more than one depth, and we can engage in interreligious encounters at any of the three Tillichian levels.

When I speak of "interreligious encounters," I have in mind anything from a Muslim's stumbling upon and watching a television program about Shinto to a committed Christian's engaging for months in regular instruction from an Advaitic Hindu guru. What makes something an interreligious encounter is the fact that more than one religious tradition is involved. This could be one's thinking about or reflecting upon religions other than one's own faith; one's studying, comparing, and teaching various religions; one's carrying on a dialogue with representatives of another religion; one's participating in activities of another tradition; or any of a host of analogous kinds of encounter.

By rethinking the threefold typology in Tillichian terms, I hope in this chapter to show the following. Most of us find that one depth of experience is more characteristic of our interreligious encounters overall, but we are by no means limited to that one level. Furthermore, the depth of any given interreligious encounter can change while it is going on, sometimes abruptly. Each of the three levels predisposes us toward one of the three attitudes, respectively, although the correlation between a given depth and its correlated attitude is not a universal and necessary connection. Other factors also come into play. Especially because we are not limited to one level in interreligious encounters, we are also not limited to just one of the three attitudes.

As this suggests, I propose a number of alterations in the typology. The change last mentioned is the most important, however. In different situations or contexts, one and the same person can be one, two, or all three of the following: a pluralist, an inclusivist, or an exclusivist. However, one can hardly adopt more than one of these attitudes at the same moment, and, as I shall explain, we sometimes adopt one or two of these attitudes in a qualified or nuanced sense.

I. Can the Typology Handle Tillich?

In relation to the typology, the strategy I have just announced is a bit aggressive. I am going to submit the familiar typology to an overhaul at the hands of Tillich's supposedly superior ideas. Tillich will show us how we can remedy the typology's deficiencies. Thus we shall be able to use it to shed light on our interreligious encounters today.

It would only be fair at least to ask, however, about an opposite strategy. What would happen if we submitted Tillich's thought to the analytic, classifying power of the typology? Can it shed fresh light on Tillich, clarify where he stands, and help with any inadequacies we find in his thought? Can the typology handle Tillich?

One quick test comes to mind. We might ask how knowledge-able interpreters have classified Tillich, and see whether their efforts in this regard have helped to make him clear.

If we thus look at a cross-section of such efforts, however, the results are anything but promising. In fact, the picture we get is almost comic. Various interpreters place Tillich all over the map. Paul Knitter characterizes him as essentially an "exclusivist."[1] John Macquarrie's judgment is similar. In Macquarrie's view, Tillich "seems to be quite as arbitrary" on this subject as Karl Barth.[2]

Yet Alan Race reaches the opposite conclusion and treats Tillich as a "pluralist,"[3] while Gavin D'Costa comes down between the ex-tremes and classifies Tillich as an "inclusivist."[4] Finally, Terence Thomas proposes to solve the puzzle by advancing a hybrid view. He argues that Tillich shifted from an inclusivist to a pluralist posi-tion late in life. As a result, Thomas concludes, we should now read the entire Tillich corpus as a pluralist text, for that is the posi-tion toward which Tillich was tending all along.[5]

---

[1]Paul Knitter, *No Other Name?* (Maryknoll NY: Orbis, 1985) 103, 106-107, 245, and 245n.47.

[2]John Macquarrie, "Christianity and Other Faiths," *Union Seminary Quarterly Review* 20 (November 1964): 43-44; idem, "Commitment and Openness," *Theology Digest* 27 (Winter 1979): 349.

[3]Alan Race, *Christians and Religious Pluralism* (Maryknoll NY: Orbis, 1983) 71, 94-97. In the second edition of this book (London: SCM Press, 1993) 177, Race buries in the middle of an endnote the acknowledgment that he may have been hasty in viewing Tillich as a pluralist, and that Tillich may be "closer to the (open) inclusivist mentality." But that is in an endnote, as I say. Race's text remains unchanged, as I cite it just above.

[4]Gavin D'Costa, *Theology and Religious Pluralism* (Oxford: Blackwell, 1986) 12, 16, 46, and 46n.1. I am indebted to Terence Thomas for calling my attention to the way Knitter, Macquarrie, Race, and D'Costa are "all over the map" in classifying Tillich. Terence Thomas, "Convergence and Divergence in a Plural World," in *Paul Tillich's Theological Legacy: Spirit and Community*, ed. Frederick J. Parrella (Berlin and New York: Walter de Gruyter, 1995) 23-29.

[5]Thomas, "Convergence and Divergence," 33-42. I view Thomas's case as quite weak, though others agree with him or have followed him. For example, see John Dourley, "Toward a Salvageable Tillich: The Implications of His Late Confession of Provincialism," paper delivered at the annual meeting of the North American Paul Tillich Society, Toronto, November 2002. For my rebuttal of such views, see James, "Tillich on 'the Absoluteness of Christianity,' " 37-42.

If we assume these men are competent interpreters, as I do, they place us before an interesting either/or. Either Tillich's thought on this issue is an ambiguous mess that defies clear interpretation, or Tillich's thought is at least potentially coherent, and the threefold typology breaks down when it comes up against a position as profound as his apparently is.

As is obvious, I have chosen the latter alternative. Thus encouraged by this quick look at the way Tillich has been interpreted, I continue with my strategy. I shall not be judging Tillich in terms of the typology. I shall be judging the typology, and trying to rethink it, in terms of Tillich's thought.

2. The "Eck Dilemma"

The main deficiency in the typology that I want to resolve is nicely epitomized in a certain dilemma. For reasons that will be apparent, I call it the "Eck dilemma," after Prof. Diana Eck of Harvard. The dilemma can arise in both a weaker and a stronger form.

(1) In its weaker form, the dilemma need be nothing worse than the suspicion that we are being inconsistent. In her *Encountering God*, Eck says that, when we use the categories of the tripartite typology, we speak "as if we are talking about three entirely different groups of people." But the attitudes epitomized in these three terms "may well be part of the ongoing dialogue within ourselves."

As Eck explains, when she comes from being involved in Hindu-Christian dialogue, for example, she understands herself "basically as a pluralist." But when she seeks to speak of her Christian faith in a new way, as when she seeks to widen and stretch her understanding of God, Christ, and the Holy Spirit, she finds herself "using what some will see as inclusivist language."

We might ask, then: Is Eck an inclusivist, a pluralist, or both? "I cannot solve this dilemma," she concludes, "but I can warmly issue an invitation to join me in thinking about it."[6] Obviously, I accept her invitation.

---

[6]Diana L. Eck, *Encountering God* (Boston: Beacon Press, 1993) 170.

(2) In its stronger form, the dilemma is felt by a number of devout people, at least in Christian circles. These people find it difficult to do justice simultaneously to the absoluteness of their own faith and the impressive relativity of all faiths. Unlike Eck, whose discomfort with this dilemma seems to be minimal, the people about whom I am speaking feel a genuine conflict between two things: (a) the propriety—and for many of these people the imperative—of an evangelizing mission on behalf of their own faith, and (b) a profound respect for the religious truth they see in other faiths, and a respect likewise for the grace and even the saintliness they discover in many of the people who belong to those faiths.

3. Differing Depths of Encounter: Three Levels at Which Knowing Takes Place

Thus far I have been stating the dilemma. As I have indicated, I believe Tillich offers a resolution of the dilemma by showing how the three attitudes identified in the typology reflect different "depths" or "levels" at which we encounter religious reality, whether we encounter that reality in other religions or within our own religious tradition.

Before launching into my discussion in this section of these *three levels* of our awareness and, in the next section, of the *two oscillating moments* in our awareness, some comments are in order. In these two sections I present what I like to call "the Tillichian mechanics of knowing." This material is likely to be a bit slower - going than the remainder of the book. Although it is basic, if a reader simply gets the general ideas, that will be sufficient for understanding what Tillich says about interreligious attitudes and encounters. Further, it is not necessary to believe Tillich has it exactly right. The issues are philosophical, and different positions are quite possible. I myself take "the Tillichian mechanics of knowing" as a *useful model* of how we know things—a model that is better than most and that helps me see things I might otherwise not notice, or would have a hard time talking about if I did.

What exactly does Tillich mean by the differing depths at which we can be engaged with religious traditions? By far the most helpful place in which he develops this idea is in a brief article published in 1955, "Participation and Knowledge: Problems of an Ontology of Cognition" (MW 1:382-89). In this little gem of an article, Tillich argues plausibly, even convincingly, that all of our cognitive intercourse with reality—our knowing things—takes place at different levels, or at different depths.

In order to follow Tillich, we need to notice how acutely aware he is that our intelligent activities are *concretely situated*. Each of our cognitive acts takes place within a given situation. It takes place in *this* particular environment, in *this* cultural-historical setting, in *these* social groups to which we belong, and within *our meaningful world*, the one we grasp and shape within the vocabulary and syntax of *this* linguistic tradition (MW 1:383, see also 384, 386).

Tillich's view here—that we know *within* some historically evolved social-cultural-linguistic context, and that the reality we know is in significant measure a construct of the corporate human mind thus located[7]—is for my purposes similar to the "internal realism" of the pragmatist philosopher, Hilary Putnam.[8] Other interpreters of religion also find Putnam helpful in this regard. Thomas Tweed appeals to him in articulating Tweed's own "locative" view.[9]

In Tillich's version of such a "locative" view, anything that we could possibly know must share with us the context within which we are located, for this context *connects* subject and object. Tillich calls this context "the situation of knowledge," or "the cognitive situation," or "the situation of encounter." As he puts it, "Subject

---

[7]For a fuller version of what I say in this immediate context, I refer to the following points that I make in chap. 3, especially on pp. 33-36, regarding the rational world that we build. We are able to "have a life" only (a) within the concrete contexts of the world we construct through reason; although (b) these contexts are full of ambiguity because we human beings construct our various life contexts *more or less* according to reason, and to a considerable extent in *irrational* ways; and further, (c) the "we" here—the "we" who construct the physical and biological *environments* in which our human world is set—include all organic and inorganic beings, and not just a few hundred generations of human beings.

[8]Hilary Putnam, *Reason, Truth and History* (Cambridge: Cambridge University Press, 1981) 49-74.

[9]Thomas A. Tweed, "On Moving Across: Translocative Religion and the Interpreter's Position," *Journal of the American Academy of Religion* 70 (2002): 255-57.

and object meet in the situation of knowledge. Both are parts of the situation" (MW 1:383, 384, 386, 389).

Of course, we are not equally connected with every object within our context. We participate more fully or less fully in any given entity within our world. And we also participate to the same degree—more fully or less fully—in the specific "situation of encounter" that connects us *with* that entity. The more completely we participate in something we know, the deeper the level at which we encounter it.

From hour to hour, if not from minute to minute, our preoccupations (our "intentions") change. As our preoccupations change from one concern to another, often the depth at which we find ourselves engaged changes. These changes of depth can be sudden, though they often come in smooth gradations. Despite the gradual way in which we may move from one level to the next, Tillich is able to mark off three different depths with a good deal of clarity (MW 1:383, 384).

The shallowest Tillichian level is the one at which "controlling knowledge" takes place. We may call it level one. Here we find the knowing subject very much separated from its object. This is the detached, highly objective kind of knowledge that we gain, for example, in the empirical sciences.

Even here, our participation in what we know, and in the situation of knowledge, is not nil. Tillich spots at least two sorts of things that connect us as cognitive subjects with what we know. (a) Through our bodily senses we receive something that stems from the object; and (b) there is also the presupposed structure of intelligent encounter itself, that is, the logical, categorical, and ontological principles that phenomenological analysis discerns.

But such ingredients do not compare to the enriched participation we have at deeper levels of cognitive encounter. The reality that links subject and object in this kind of detached knowledge is thin and minimal, as is the subject's participation in the object (MW 1:384-85).

At the second level, or middle depth, we experience something of a balance between (a) participating in the object—and participating in the context or situation of encounter that *embraces* subject and object—and (b) separating from that object, as we grasp it conceptually.

This is the level at which we know life processes as a matter of "insight" into our own life and into the lives of others. Or, more precisely, our awareness of *our own* life process is a matter of insight, whereas the awareness we attain as we enter partly into the lives of *others* is a matter of "empathy."

More broadly seen, this middle level is the level at which we "understand." It is the depth in which we understand and interpret the manifold expressions of the human spirit, in the arts, in scientific projects, in mastering and using a language, in social movements, in political causes, and in other humane spheres.

Lastly, there is the deepest, or third, level. At this level we are aware of things with which our lives are so totally wrapped up that we are grasped, through these things and along with these things, at a depth beyond that at which any encountered realities stand opposite us as objects. This third level is existential knowledge. Religious knowledge is existential in this sense. It is our awareness of values, causes, imperatives, and realities that shape and determine who and what we are in our deepest selves.

4. Oscillation through Time:
Separative versus Participative Moments

According to Tillich's analysis, our knowledge at each level takes place through time in an oscillation of alternating moments. He appears to think of this oscillation as quite rapid, as too fast for us to perceive it. A predominantly participating moment is followed by a predominantly separating moment, then vice versa, and so on.

In none of these microinstants is either the moment of participation or the moment of separation completely absent. The difference between the two kinds of moment is that in one moment participative *union predominates*, whereas in the next moment separative *objectification predominates*, then the opposite, and so on (MW 1:389).

The oscillation we are examining at this point is not the same as something I mentioned several paragraphs above, namely, our shifting our attention from one subject to another. Those changes in preoccupation, or changes in "intention," typically take place in terms of hours and minutes. By contrast, Tillich seems clearly to be thinking of the successive phases in this oscillation as like vibrations that follow one another so fast we do not perceive them. Rather than our perceiving them, they are the means whereby we perceive anything at all.

This makes sense in that it is the difference between the two phases that enables us to do the two opposite-tending things, namely, to separate-and-objectify, on the one hand, and to participate-and-have-union-with, on the other hand.

It will clarify things if we take another look at the deepest or religious-existential level. At this depth of our awareness, the extent of our participation in objects—and the extent of our participation in the situation of our *encountering* these objects—is so overwhelming that the predominantly separative-objectifying moments are weaker, less intense, and less marked. Still, as I have already observed, these separating moments never totally disappear. If these objectifying moments were totally dissolved in the vibrations or oscillations of our separating-participating consciousness, there would be no objective contents in our awareness. There would be nothing "over against us" that we were conscious of and making cognitive judgments *about*.[10]

But objects do in fact continue to "be there" for us human beings in this deepest level, just as they do in the other two levels of encounter. They continue to be there by virtue of the incessant, pulsing return of the predominantly separating-objectifying moments. These moments, we recall, are ingredient in every instance of cognitive awareness, even in unfolding episodes of religious awareness.

What is it that is distinctive about the objects of our distinctly religious consciousness? If we look at the truly central ones—that

---

[10]In such a situation, as Tillich views it, interactions between us and items in our environment would continue. We would even be consciously aware of them in the way nonhuman animals are. After all, both we and they have "inner awareness" (ST 3:20-21). But, in Tillich's model of human mentality, we would not be sufficiently "separated" from things in our environment—inwardly separated from them in conscious "intention," that is—that we could grasp particulars as instances of universals, make true-or-false judgments about them, reason about them, and deal abstractly and in a truly creative way with them.

is, the ones that have gained the power to orient us and to exert a life-shaping claim upon us, as in the case of Jesus the Christ for Christians, or the Buddha for Buddhists—we see that these objects have a unique function. They are the means whereby the mothering ground of, and the fatherly constraint within, all that is real grasp us and claim us. In a word—in a Tillichian word—these objects are religious symbols.[11]

In and through these symbolic realities, the transcendent gets at us—the transcendent that, at least for Western religions, is God. We cannot directly grasp and objectify this ultimate ground of our being. But it grasps us. In fact, it is *always* grasping, sustaining, and constraining us, though we are usually not conscious that we are *being* grasped in this way. Because it grasps us from beyond the objective world that we finite subjects grasp and shape and help to construct, we can say—in a Tillichian phrase—that it grasps us "at a level beyond the subject-object opposition."[12]

---

[11]Tillich's idea of the religious symbol should become clear as I proceed here, but I may perhaps call attention to my fuller discussion of it on pp. 40-42 of the preceding chapter. Pertinent there are both my discussion of the "symbolic" character, and of the "nonrational" character, of what I call there "the reconciling act."

[12]As already mentioned in the preface and introduction above, I have a huge difference with Tillich at this point. That difference, spelled out fully in chap. 9 below (pp. 141-58), is pinpointed by the following question. In our religious encounters, is the divine or Eternal Thou "there," encountering us in an ultimately real way, even though our objectifications of this Thou are always inadequate, and are even misleading, more or less, inasmuch as we participate in the Eternal Thou, and it in us, as well as encountering the Eternal Thou?

To that question I say: Yes, the divine Thou is *steadily and ultimately* "there," meeting us *through* things that are or that could be symbolic for us, though we often are not sufficiently responsive to the Eternal Thou to be aware of it. To the same question Tillich gives a "no" answer. For him, what I intuit as "the Eternal Thou" is "there" for us in a dialectical yes-and-no way in which the participative moment cancels this "thereness" as quickly as the objectifying moment sets it up, while, vice versa, the objectifying moment sets it up as quickly as the participative moment cancels it. In a context in which he explains this situation, Tillich speaks of the "oscillation between the setting up and the destruction of the religious object" (MW 4:264, cf. 263-69). Contrast finite entities. For Tillich, they cease to be if they *lose* all over-againstness, all substance-hood or thingness, whereas the Eternal Thou ceases to be what it is insofar as it *gains* over-againstness and thinghood—insofar as it becomes "a being."

5. Knowing Religions at the First Level: Contextual Pluralism

What happens as we confront religions or their representatives at the differing levels that Tillich identifies? When we operate at the level of empirical, objective, controlling knowledge, something inevitably gets lost. In this mood of detached mastery, the vaulting splendor and the awesome, fascinating quality of these great symbolic forms of life tend either to drop out of the picture or to be rendered as abstractions—as phenomenologically intuitable structures, for example.

The details regarding the religions that we master in this exterioristic manner virtually beg to be given comparative treatment alongside other, similar phenomena. In the soil of this kind of encounter with other faiths, implications of parity and equal worth grow like flowers—or "like weeds," as we might prefer to say, if we happen to be ill-disposed toward pluralism. In other words, grappling with religions at this first level is a strong predisposer toward a pluralist way of assessing religions.

In the light of what I have just said, I conclude that there is a correlation between a pluralistic attitude and interreligious encounters at the first, most detached, and most objective level of our experience and our knowledge.

This level-one correlation does not mean, however, that all who spend time mastering, teaching, or interpreting religions in a level-one, objective way must become pluralists. Two examples will show that this does not necessarily happen, two examples from among hundreds of possible examples.

My first example is S. Mark Heim. His 1995 book, *Salvations*, is written overall from a Christian inclusivist point of view that explicitly *opposes* the pluralist project. Yet one of Heim's main purposes is to show how different salvations, or different religious ends, are envisioned and facilitated by the various religions. And that purpose requires that much of his book be written, not only with interpretive empathy for other faiths, but also with impartial objectivity, or with what I am describing as objective, level-one attention to empirical detail.[13]

My second example is Tillich himself. He recognizes deep structural, thematic, and substantive commonalities between Christian faith and other religions, and is sharply critical of efforts to present a theology of the history of religions that fails to affirm divine revelation in all religious experience (ST 1:220-21, 221n.). We find discourse of this pluralist kind even within Tillich's *Systematic Theology*, which is Christian, of course.

In fact, it is a matter of principle for Tillich that a predominantly pluralist discourse will characterize a recurring component of his theology. To see what is involved, we need to be aware that Tillich's theology contains five main parts—Reason and Revelation, Being and God, Existence and Christ, Life and the Spirit, and History and the Kingdom of God (ST 1:66-68)—and that in each of these five parts Tillich makes three kinds of "move." The first move within each of these parts is an essentially philosophical elaboration of a cluster of existential questions (ST 1:63-64). It is not religiously partisan. Thus it would be pluralist, except that it does not deal with many data that are religious in the usual sense of the term. The concluding move in each part of Tillich's system elaborates the answers given in the Christian message to the questions previously developed. This third move is normatively Christian, of course.

It is the "middle third" in each part of Tillich's system that is of interest at the moment. The kind of move Tillich makes in this middle third is a historical, empirically descriptive, interpretive, or phenomenological treatment of material from the history of religions (ST 1:106-31, 211-35; ST 2:79-96; ST 3:111-61, 348-61).

Tillich is forthright that his selection and shaping of this religious material assumes criteria that he will shortly present in his third or normative move (ST 1:66). But even the most fastidious pluralist will hardly be able to take exception to the way Tillich actually treats the material, not least because he finds both the

---

[13]S. Mark Heim, *Salvations: Truth and Difference in Religions* (Maryknoll NY: Orbis Books, 1995) 6-10, and cf. chap. 5 and most of part two, 129-210, in Heim's book.

truth of revelation, and its saving or transforming power, in all religion.[14]

Thus far I have spoken of how Tillich proceeds within his theological work, which is Christian, of course. When we move beyond his theology to his discussions of religion, and of various religions, or of encounters among religions, we find Tillich speaking in an evenhanded, "level-one" way that seems for the most part studiously to avoid privileging one religion over another.[15] This is notably true of Tillich's addresses during the last eight years or so of his life.[16]

As in the case of Heim, however, it does not follow that Tillich is a pluralist. In fact, in what follows I expect to show that Tillich can also be seen as inclusivist and exclusivist, in certain important senses. Even so, the palpably pluralist character of much of the discourse of Heim, Tillich, and many others is interesting. To account for it, I propose the category of *contextual pluralism*.

A "contextual pluralist," in the sense I intend, is thus someone who adopts a pluralist attitude in certain contexts, although this person's more characteristic attitude is not pluralist. In the case of both Heim and Tillich, the kind of context in which they are pluralist is the situation in which these two thinkers accept the

---

[14]A clear example is Tillich's religion-wide treatment of "revelation." ST 1:106-31.

[15]For example, see Paul Tillich, *Christianity and the Encounter of the World Religions* (New York and London: Columbia University Press, 1963); see also n. 19 below and Tillich, *The Encounter of Religions and Quasi-Religions*, ed. Terence Thomas (Lewiston/Queenston/Lampeter: Edwin Mellen Press, 1990). Within these texts and within the "middle third" of his theology, we find Tillich speaking in this "level-one way," as I have said. But in such contexts we also find him speaking more often in the "level-two way" that I am about to explain in my text above. For this reason, Tillich may not be the best example of the level-one correlation with pluralism. His "nonpartisan" treatments of religion are a useable example, however, even if not the best example. I am convinced, of course, that the correlation itself stands.

[16]Though I think Terence Thomas misses some things, it is still a revealing fact that he can read these late essays as straightforwardly pluralist. Thomas, "Convergence and Divergence," 33-42.

obligations and fill the role of an impartial, objective, "level-one" analyst of religions.[17]

6. Encountering Religion at the Second and Third Levels

We turn to the middle level of our encounters with religious reality. At this second level, we find ourselves entering empathetically into life forms, sometimes even into strange life forms. Or, more precisely, we enter *partially* into these forms, and they enter *partially* into us. The result is that we live partly in them, while they live at least a tiny part of their life in us.

This kind of "partly growing together with the other," as I would describe it, can happen even with hitherto alien persons, alien practices, alien outlooks, and alien institutions. Or such growing together can happen, I should say, *if* we have continuing contact with these alien forms over a long enough period of time that some degree of storied-historical togetherness puts in its appearance. The beginnings of this kind of thing must have been taking place in 1960 as Tillich engaged in a series of dialogues with leading Buddhists in Japan. Certainly this was happening if these dialogues were taking place at Tillich's second level of encounter, as Tillich's accounts of these encounters strongly suggest.[18]

In order to clarify the relation between the second and third levels, we might reflect upon an imaginary scenario. It is an extremely unlikely scenario, but it is one we could extrapolate from Tillich's Japan experience. In a very extended, level-two dialogue between persons of differing faiths, it would be possible (at least in principle) that their level-two experience of "partly growing together with each other" could be punctuated—it could even be commandeered—by a gradual manifestation or a sudden breakthrough of the holy ultimate. That would be a level-three event, of course.

---

[17]As we shall see in chap. 6 (pp. 95-96), there is another kind of context in which a Tillichian would be a contextual pluralist—even at the third and deepest level of experience!—namely, when the person involved is strongly mystical in piety, or is empathizing in a very real way with strongly mystical piety.

[18]See "Japan, 1960: Paulus Writes," in Hannah Tillich, *From Place to Place* (New York: Stein and Day, 1976) 93-114.

For such a thing to happen among people of different religious traditions, however, one can hardly imagine the enormous amount of prior preparation that would be required. This preparation would involve not merely some prior conditions in the personal lives of the individuals involved. It would also require some kind of developments earlier, probably much earlier, in the cultures and religiously symbolic traditions that have birthed and formed these individuals. If, against all odds, this preparation were in place, however, and if a revelatory manifestation or breakthrough took place—and if it were more than a flash of lightning followed by the dark—then a new "correlation of revelation" would have been constituted. And this new correlation would involve some freshly configured symbolic contents (ST 1:126-28).

For example, were this to happen in the context of some years or decades of ongoing Christian-Buddhist dialogue, one would expect to see—within the collective psyche, the shared outlook, and the ritualized action of the group involved—some kind of fusion of Buddhist and Christian symbolisms. And, of course, the dialogue group that was overtaken by such a transforming break-through would be constituted, precisely by that development, as a new religious community. Such an event would be a revelatory experience.[19]

But such manifestations and breakthroughs are not only unlikely in the extreme. They are also not what interfaith dialogue is about. I have invoked my imaginary scenario in order to make

---

[19]"A living religion comes to life only if a new revelatory experience appears." MW 5:315. The text in MW was first published as Tillich's *Christianity and the Encounter of the World Religions*, Bampton Lectures 14 (1962) (but delivered in the fall of 1961) (New York and London: Columbia University Press, 1963) 67. It was republished with different pagination in 1994 under virtually the same title (this "second edition" dropped the second "the")—but with a foreword by Krister Stendahl and the addition of a fifth Tillich lecture, his final public lecture, "The Significance of the History of Religions for the Systematic Theologian"—in the Fortress Texts in Modern Theology series (Minneapolis: Fortress Press). In the 1994 edition the quotation appears on page 42. Henceforth I cite this work in all three editions in the following format: Tillich, *Christianity and the Encounter of World Religions* (1963) 67; (1994) 42; MW 5:315.

clear the difference between a level-two and a level-three encounter with religion.

7. Correlating Levels and Attitudes

If we return to the more usual kind of interfaith dialogue, we shall find that it normally takes place in a middle-level encounter between us and our religious "other." Even without the dramatic or transforming kind of level-three breakthrough that I described in my fictional scenario, our level-two "understanding" interactions with other faiths are likely to uncover elements in these religions that are similar to the things that shape and determine our own reality in depth.

When we detect these similar or analogous elements, we begin to understand how the transforming truth that grasps us in our faith is making itself felt—with what degree of clarity and strength we may not be sure—in the faith of the other person, also. This is clearly an inclusivist insight. The key point is that we sense in the other tradition some of the religious power and truth that, for us, are normatively present in our own religious tradition.

Thus we have a correlation of some moment between level-two interreligious encounters and an inclusivist attitude. Previously, in section 5 of this chapter, we saw a correlation—though not a necessary and universal link—between our level-one interreligious encounters and a pluralist attitude.

What is to be said about the remaining level, the third and most profound? At this level, we are grasped by reality at its deepest and most embracing. At this depth the ground of our being and the ground of all meaning get at us through religious symbols such as the Buddha nature, or God's covenant with my people Israel, or the unity of all things in Brahman, or the living Lord who gave himself that I might have abundant life.

In and through these realities we are grasped at a level beyond the level at which these realities are simply objects for us as subjects. "Who we are" and "how we shall live" are so tied up with these realities that it would be a preposterous trivialization to think that we could swap one of them for another. Thus—with the exception of the few cases that are predominantly "mystical," an exception with which I shall deal in chapter 6[20]—when we speak out of and for our experience at this third or existential depth of interreligious encounter, we will not be able to affirm salvation or ultimate fulfillment within the symbolism of any other religion than the one in whose beneficent grip we sense ourselves then to be. And it would also be a trivialization of the situation if we undertook, at this level of an interreligious encounter, to rank the "top forty" religious symbols in the world as all on a par.

I think it fair to call what we experience in this way an exclusivist *tendency*. In some cases, we would even call it an exclusivist *impulse*. Whatever we call it, tendency or impulse, should we also call it "exclusivism"? For two reasons, I believe we should not. First, the tendency I am talking about is something we *feel*, or something we are *moved by*, whereas exclusivism is an attitude in the sense of a stance or a position that we *adopt*. The fact that we feel the tendency does not mean, by itself, that we will adopt the attitude.

And second, the exclusivist tendency I have just described is something that is (a) "positive with a limit," whereas the exclusivist attitude involves (b) an explicit negative, or a denial.

(a) "Positively" the tendency means we affirm salvation within our own faith, of course, whereas the "limit" means that we *do not* affirm salvation in the other religion that is involved in the encounter. In some cases this "limit" amounts to our *inability* to affirm salvation in another religious tradition.

By contrast with the (a) item just described—I call it a *tendency*—(b) the *attitude* of exclusivism involves an explicit negative claim. It is the claim that salvation is not to be found anywhere else than in one's own religion. Exclusivism proper is an attitude that involves the denial that there is any ultimate fulfillment in another faith, whereas the exclusivist tendency may be no more than simply the nonaffirmation of salvation elsewhere—though in

---

[20]On pp. 95-96, 103-105 below, I explain that, on Tillich's understanding of the matter, in the small minority of cases in which a person's piety is more mystical than it is sacramental or ethical, that person will most likely sense *pluralist* tendencies at the third level, whereas (as I say in the text above) the tendency usually felt in the large majority of level-three interreligious encounters is *exclusivist*.

some cases it will also be the *inability to affirm* salvation elsewhere. This may appear to be a rather fine distinction, this distinction between (a) "nonaffirmation" or "inability to affirm," on the one hand, and (b) "denial," on the other hand. But as we shall see later, the distinction should be illuminating and useful.

Given the exclusivist tendency or impulse that I have described, I believe we may say that there is a significant correlation between third-level religious experience and an exclusivist attitude. Or, more precisely, I believe that is the main correlation. I have acknowledged a small exception in the case of strongly mystical piety, an exception that I will discuss in chapter 6.

Nevertheless, this correlation does not mean that level-three religious experience by itself will make us exclusivistic in attitude. Other factors are involved, and some of them will abet this tendency toward exclusivism, while others of these factors will restrain this tendency toward exclusivism.

For example, in social groups, cultures, or subcultures that have been steeped in doctrines and beliefs characteristic of missionary Christianity, deeper level religious experience will easily issue in exclusivistic convictions, or will easily confirm exclusivist convictions that may already have been instilled in the individual.

And, to take an opposite example, for many of the people nurtured even within such traditions, the effects of exclusivistic doctrine can be held in check if these people's awareness of various religions has been impregnated with level-one analyses and explanations (perhaps in a college course on Islam), or if these people's experience has been enriched by level-two empathy and understanding in relation to other faith traditions and their representatives.

Although Tillich did not live to address the topic I have examined in this section, he documents most of the key points in the following passage from his *Systematic Theology*. He is speaking primarily of an Eastern religion, but it is clear that he intends his remarks to have general application.

> One can learn many things about strange religions and cultures by means of detached observation [level one] and even more through empathetic understanding [level two]. But neither way

leads to the central experience of an Asian religion for one who has grown [sic] within the Christian-humanist civilization of the West. . . . [O]ne should be warned by the statement of a great interpreter of Chinese ideas that after thirty years of living among the Chinese he has just begun to understand a little of their Spiritual life. The only authentic way to it is through actual participation [level three]. (ST 3:141; bracketed text added)

Tillich's point here is not to forbid people from seeking to participate deeply in another religion. That would be foreign to his overall approach.[21] His point rather is to make it clear how demanding such level-three participation is. But in the process, he also describes what we can know, and how we come to know it, in first- and in second-level interreligious encounters, also.

8. Different Attitudes within the Same Person

How does all this illuminate the Eck dilemma from which we set out early in this chapter? Most people who have been deeply religious themselves, have probably had at least some fleeting experience with religion at all three of Tillich's levels of knowing. But not equally at all levels. Because of such differences, plus other differences, we are likely to find ourselves drawn only toward one, or perhaps toward two of the attitudes in the typology. Diana Eck tells us, as we have seen, that she engages in both inclusivist and pluralist ways of thinking and speaking.

---

[21]Tillich himself sought to participate in Buddhism in his trip to Japan in 1960. In addition, some formative features of his thought encourage such a quest—though with an important proviso. On Tillich's principles, when we seek to participate in hitherto alien religious experience, we are supported by the drive toward a grand telos, as it were, within the overall religious experience of humankind. This is a drive toward an all-inclusive unification of diverse religious elements. See Paul Tillich, "The Philosophy of Religion," trans. James Luther Adams and Charles W. Fox, in *What Is Religion?* (New York: Harper & Row, 1969) 88-101, German original at MW 4:150-57. However, if we are drawn toward this telos in a way that is in keeping with the nature of that unifying telos itself, we will not seek it by attenuating the concrete richness of our experience *within our own religious tradition.* See ST 1:241 and Paul Tillich, *Dynamics of Faith* (New York: Harper & Brothers, 1957) 48-54.

But what if our awareness of the total religious enterprise of humankind is well informed and sophisticated, our understanding of that enterprise highly perceptive, and our sharing in some forms of that enterprise extraordinarily profound? In that case, we might well find ourselves to be, as I believe Tillich found himself to be, all three of these things: a pluralist, an inclusivist, *and* an exclusivist—although in respectively different degrees in this or that particular context.

Further, our adopting two if not all three of these attitudes during this or that span of time will probably not cancel out the fact that we shall feel more at home in one of them. We will normally have what might be called a "baseline attitude," that is, an attitude that is most characteristic of our encounters with other faiths overall. In Tillich's case, as I explain in chapter 7, I believe this baseline attitude is inclusivism, in particular, something I shall call "reciprocal inclusivism."

Let me try to show how we may very plausibly have two or more of the three attitudes. I am going to make this effort as existential as you, the reader, will allow. If you and I have been nurtured and deeply shaped, you by Buddhism, and I by Christianity; and if you know and understand a lot about Christianity, and I know and understand a lot about Buddhism; then at the detached level of objective assessment, or at the interpretive level of empathetic understanding, each of us can make quite a case for the equal worth, or for the comparable vitality, of the other's religion.

But let us move for a moment beyond the usual level of dialogue toward something deeper. That is, let us imagine a situation in which one of us realizes that we can be the means whereby the other person will receive or achieve something that may answer that person's deepest existential needs. And let us by all means imagine this as a situation in which any "evangelization" that took place, in whichever direction, would be totally voluntary and consensual: that is, the other one of us *wishes us* to be of help in this way.

If such a situation were to develop, then you, a Buddhist, are not likely to speak a compassionate word to me in terms of Christian symbols and concepts; nor am I, a Christian, likely to speak a caring word to you in terms of Buddhist concepts and symbols. Instead, we shall each reach out with what we know existentially as transforming, and can therefore share as healing. That is all we have to offer at this level of deep calling to deep.

The potentially exclusivist implications of what I have just said are patent. And for some of the people who might participate in a scenario of this kind, the experience would become *actually* exclusivist. However, if these people are the kinds of people I have described in my particular, imaginary scenario, their exclusivism will be "practical" or "contextual."

The exclusivism is "practical" and "contextual" in this sense: for the praxis that is called for at *this* level of engagement, and in *this* concrete time and place, other ways of salvation or existential healing are *excluded*. Nevertheless, each of the fictional individuals in my scenario appreciates the other's religion in inclusivist and in pluralist terms, as we have seen.

The next chapter deals with the "contextual exclusivism" that I have briefly described here.[22]

9. A Confirming Philosophical Parallel in Nicholas Rescher

In trying to make sense of the persistent diversity of philosophical positions, Nicholas Rescher has proposed a position that he calls "orientational pluralism"—although he quickly tells us that the "obverse" of such pluralism is "orientational monism."[23] To the extent that Rescher's orientational pluralism/monism is convinc-

---

[22]As I explain there, the fact that this exclusivism is contextual involves three points. (a) The baseline attitude is not exclusivist. (b) The person is ready and able to adopt an exclusivist attitude in the appropriate contexts, but only in such contexts. (c) The person can conceive the possibility that, in other contexts, some faith other than their own might serve as the only available vehicle of ultimate fulfillment—or of some measure of such fulfillment, in any case.

[23]Owen C. Thomas drew my attention to Rescher's position both in his response to the 1995 paper in which I first presented several of the ideas in chaps. 4–7 (see my acknowledgments), and in an essay of his to which he directed me. Owen C. Thomas, "Religious Plurality and Contemporary Philosophy: A Critical Survey," *Harvard Theological Review* 87 (1994): 197-213, cf. esp. 210-13.

ing, it tends strongly to confirm both my level-one and my level-three correlations, and also to confirm the fact that most of us adopt more than one of the three attitudes in the familiar typology.

Rescher's orientational pluralism, to speak only of that side of his position, points to something we experience in philosophical study when we step back from actually doing philosophy in order to try to understand the work of the philosophical community as a whole. From that vantage point, we see that philosophy will never be able rationally to constrain agreement on its main problems. Rather, mutually incompatible positions on the philosophical issues will always be tenable—*rationally* tenable.

Philosophical pluralism of this kind is nicely analogous to the pluralist tendency of the "level-one" religion scholar who deals theoretically, or in a detached empirical way, with various religions. But up to this point, as Rescher views the matter, a person is not so much *doing* philosophy as *surveying* it, and understanding it as an aggregate human enterprise.

What happens if we step up to the plate and take a swing at actually doing philosophy? That is to say, What happens if we try to solve a specific philosophical problem? Or, to take the analogous question in religion, What happens if we plunge into the actual experience and practice of religion?

According to Rescher, when we apply ourselves to resolving a philosophical problem, we inevitably orient ourselves as a monist. We are determined to articulate the single most adequate solution. Nor is this egomania or obstinacy on our part. In order to do philosophical work, he argues, we must commit ourselves to one or another of several possible orderings of cognitive values— importance, centrality, priority, and the like—and when we do that, the commitment we thus make, together with our social-cultural-historical location and our native talent, gives us a single "value orientation" and a perspective. From this standpoint there will be, for us and for anyone thus situated, one optimum judgment to be reached.

As Rescher summarizes at one point, "The individual is inherently monistic. He has, or can develop, only a single value framework and must arrive at one set of weights and priorities." By contrast, "The community . . . is inherently pluralistic. There is no such thing as a communal-value posture."[24]

Religious exclusivism is analogous here to Rescher's orientational monism. We feel the tug of this exclusivist orientation when we are drawn into the third or existential level of our dealings with religion, that is, when we are *involved in the practice* of religion, and are no longer just spectators.

10. Conclusion

When the familiar tripartite typology is reconceived in terms of the differing depths of experience in the Tillichian way I have suggested, it becomes clear how one and the same person may be, at almost the same time, and depending upon the context, any one, or any two, or indeed all three—an exclusivist, an inclusivist, or a pluralist.

A Tillichian position such as this appears to be able to do justice both to the absoluteness of faith and the relativity of faiths; and it is able to do this in a way that can satisfy broadly sophisticated world citizens as well as partisans of an evangelizing or missionary enterprise.

In that way we are able to deal with the Eck dilemma, even in its stronger form. Devout people not only *may* affirm the absoluteness of their faith, but at least in certain contexts, and at the deepest level of their experience, they will quite appropriately feel *impelled* to affirm the absoluteness of their faith. And they can do that without their necessarily raising claims of objectively empirical superiority for their own religion, and without their ceasing to be open to the truth of other faiths, and even to some of the transforming power in those faiths.

---

[24]Nicholas Rescher, *The Strife of Systems* (Pittsburgh: University of Pittsburgh Press, 1985) 145, cf. xi, 147, 178, 190, 265-67.

Chapter 5

Contextual Exclusivism

In the previous chapter the category of "contextual exclusivism" emerged almost unbidden as we dealt with an imaginary Buddhist-Christian dialogue.[1] Our purpose there was to show that one and the same person could adopt two, or even all three, of the interreligious attitudes in the typology.

An exclusivist attitude is one of those three attitudes, of course; but that posed a problem that I passed over in silence. It is virtually inconceivable that a real exclusivist would get involved in the kind of dialogue I described there in the first place. In my fictional scenario, the parties are not only well informed about each other's religion, which some exclusivists might be, of course. They are also mutually forthcoming with pluralistic affirmation, and with inclusivist understanding. People who would participate in such a dialogue might be pluralist, or they might be inclusivist, but they could hardly be exclusivist!

That is to say, *only in certain contexts* would such people be drawn into adopting an exclusivist attitude, including the kind of context I described. At most they would be "contextual exclusivists."

As these remarks suggest, a contextual exclusivist is marked by three characteristics. (a) The person's baseline attitude in interreligious encounters is not exclusivist. (b) It is only in certain contexts, and in encounters of considerable depth, that this person gives relatively free rein to an exclusivist tendency; but the contextual exclusivist is ready and able to adopt an exclusivist attitude in such contexts. And (c) the contextual exclusivist can conceive the possibility that, in other contexts—contexts besides the ones that evoke an exclusivist response in them—another faith besides their own might serve as the vehicle of ultimate fulfillment, or as the vehicle of some measure of such fulfillment. Perhaps that other faith is the only available option. Perhaps it is so dominant in that

---

[1]See pp. 70-71 above.

setting that no other religion can be effective with those people in that particular time and place.

So far as the name of this proposed category is concerned, it will sometimes be illuminating to call it "practical exclusivism" as well as "contextual exclusivism." The reason is that, when we put aside all mere theory and attend to the *praxis* that is called for in certain in-depth encounters, our actions *in such contexts* will proceed in the recognition that ultimate healing or fulfillment is "at hand" only in the concreteness and symbolism of the one religion that we sense to be effective then and there, namely, our own religion.

This proposed category of contextual exclusivism is important for the position I am developing in this book. To the extent that it stands scrutiny, it shows how one's commitment to the missionary and evangelizing expansion of one's own religion is compatible with one's appreciating other faiths, and even appropriating some of the life, truth, and health that is to be found in them.

I. Tillich as Resource for Evangelical Theology

Notwithstanding the fact that we are talking here only about a qualified kind of exclusivism, contextual exclusivism, it is important that exclusivism of *some* assertive kind is conceivable on the basis of Tillich's thought—and *called for* by his thought, as I see the matter. One reason among others why this is important is that it shows us a side of Tillich that can be a resource for the large company of evangelical theologians. Or better, it shows us a side of Tillich that can be a resource for evangelical theologians of a more moderate stripe, in any case.[2]

---

[2]See Gregory A. Boyd and Paul R. Eddy, *Across the Spectrum: Understanding Issues in Evangelical Theology* (Grand Rapids MI: Baker Book House, 2002) chap. 12, "The Destiny of the Unevangelized Debate," 178-92. Any of the four positions except the "restrictivist" could easily draw upon Tillich's thought at this point. If it is true that restrictivists constitute a majority of evangelicals (and they may not), that would mean that only a minority of evangelicals could make use of Tillich at this point. But, in fact, even some restrictivists could find Tillich useful on this topic.

As a matter of fact, this particular side of Tillich is only one of at least three features of his thought that evangelicals could draw upon with profit. In chapter 8 I shall deal at some length with a second of these features. That is Tillich's doctrine that, for Christians, final revelation and the center of history are vested in Jesus received as the Christ (cf. ST 3:364-82).

The third such feature of Tillich's thought is something I do not systematically pursue in this book. I do touch upon it significantly in several places, however, both in section 5 of this chapter below, and in chapter 8 as well. This third feature is the deep biblical structure of Tillich's thought—"biblical" in the sense of the Christian Bible. My conviction is that, if evangelicals undertook serious study of Tillich, it could help them become as biblical as they intend to be.[3]

The present chapter is concerned, however, with the first of these three features of Tillich's thought. The chapter's purpose, that is to say, is to explain in Tillichian terms the contextual exclusivism I have just described, and to explore some of its connections, implications, and possibilities—including its promise for evangelical theology.

But why is it that more people have not seen the propriety of exclusivism, at least in certain contexts, as Tillich has? In the next section, I offer the hypothesis that these other people may not have been as consistently aware as Tillich was that the central thing religion does is to bring about existential healing.

---

[3]In a 1994 paper ("How Postmodernism, Even Tillich, Can Help Evangelicals," presented at the Third Annual Wheaton Theology Conference, Wheaton College, Wheaton IL, April 1994), I argue that Tillich's theology is one means whereby evangelicals can get over a major obstacle to their being as biblical as they would like to be. Standing in their way at present is a "conspiracy" between (1) a post-Newtonian, modern, individualistic ontology, and (2) a one-sidedly Acts-oriented appropriation of the New Testament. This (metaphorical) conspiracy stifles a priori for most evangelicals certain motifs that are well rendered in Tillich, namely, some important corporate and concretely mystical motifs in the way salvation in Christ is understood in the Pauline and Johannine parts of the New Testament (but not in the Book of Acts, whose strengths lie elsewhere). I make the argument of my 1994 paper clearer and more aggressive in two endeavors I describe on p. 8, n. 14, above.

2. What Religion Does—
Except When It Goes on Vacation

A famous saying by Ludwig Wittgenstein opens up the issue just posed, and also provides a theme for dealing with it. He writes, "philosophical problems arise when language goes on holiday."[4] We might restate Wittgenstein's point by saying that it is only when we actually use language so that it is "doing its thing" for us, that we can understand it aright. If we try to step outside of language, stop it in its tracks, and force it to go "on vacation," we are liable to confuse ourselves and come to very inadequate conclusions as to what language is, and what it does.

The same seems to be true when we take a vacation from religion and force it to go on holiday in relation to us. We are likely to confuse ourselves and come to very inadequate conclusions about what religion is and what it does. But what exactly is religion doing when it is *not* on vacation?

For Tillich it is an enormous part of the answer that, when religion is "doing its thing," the thing it is doing is healing. It is bringing about existential healing.[5] "[A] religion without healing or saving power," Tillich contends, "is irrelevant."[6] Certainly, religion can do more than that. It can energize, motivate, celebrate, inspire, enrich, deepen, uplift, hallow, and bless, even when no ills or hurts are the conscious focus of what people are feeling at the time. But a living religion cannot do *less* than heal, particularly if one understands "healing" in a broad sense, as I am doing.

---

[4]Ludwig Wittgenstein, *Philosophical Investigations: The English Text of the Third Edition*, trans. G. E. M. Anscombe (New York: Macmillan, 1958) 19.

[5]"In some way and on some level, every human being is longing for a new reality in contrast to the distorted reality in which he is living." Paul Tillich, "Missions and World History," in *The Theology of the Christian Mission*, ed. Gerald H. Anderson (New York: McGraw-Hill, 1961) 286. This is the edition I have used, although this Tillich essay first appeared as "The Theology of Missions," in *Occasional Bulletin of the Missionary Research Library* (New York) 5 (10 August 1954): 6-16 (not seen by me). It is unfortunate this essay was not included in MW.

[6]MW 315. For this reference I am indebted to Dr. Karin Grau of Vaihingen/Enz, Germany. See Karin Grau, "Salvation as Cosmic Healing in Tillich," *North American Paul Tillich Society Newsletter* 28/3 (Summer 2002): 24.

Further, I understand "healing" to include both consoling and comforting, on the one hand, and the important curative *side* of energizing, motivating, celebrating, and the like, on the other hand.

In keeping with this, the *hypothesis I propose in this section* is as follows. Those who fail to recognize the propriety of exclusivism, at least in certain important contexts, have not interpreted religion sufficiently from a perspective that is located *within*, engaged *with*, and speaking *for* (or at least *out of*) the healing enterprise—the healing enterprise that belongs to the very essence of religion.

One might object to my hypothesis by pointing out that there are able interpreters of religion who emphasize the healing function of religion, although they are opposed to exclusivism.[7] John Hick is an example. He gives great weight to world religions as soteriological vehicles that transform persons existentially from self-centeredness to Reality-centeredness. Yet he also advances what he calls "the pluralistic hypothesis,"[8] and is very much opposed to the idea of the absoluteness of Christianity that expresses itself in an often-destructive Christian exclusivism.[9]

I do not believe my hypothesis in this section is vulnerable to this objection. A difference of cognitive levels is involved. The interpretation of religions done by Hick and others is carried out at the first or second cognitive level, or, more often, at a combination of these levels. The interest that drives these interpretations is the concern to render religions understandable, and to do so by describing and explaining what goes on in them. That is to say, a *descriptive-explanatory interest* gives birth to the kind of intelligibility these interpreters seek, and find.

By contrast, the hypothesis I am defending here speaks of the way we find it meaningful to *practice* a religion. At its heart, that is a level-three undertaking. Moreover, my hypothesis speaks of

---

[7]John Thatamanil (see my acknowledgments, above) made this objection to an earlier version of this hypothesis.

[8]John Hick, *An Interpretation of Religion* (New Haven CT and London: Yale University Press, 1989) 29-35, 233-51; cf. 240, 361, 376.

[9]John Hick, "The Non-Absoluteness of Christianity," in *The Myth of Christian Uniqueness*, ed. John Hick and Paul F. Knitter (Maryknoll NY: Orbis Books, 1987) 16-36.

the way we find it meaningful to be engaged in the *healing or saving function* of a religion. In this situation, it is a *therapeutic-soteriological interest* that gives birth to the kind of intelligibility we seek, and perhaps find. This is not the interest to describe, to explain, or to analyze. Per se, it is not even the interest to understand or to appreciate a religion. It is the *concern to be made whole*— and often it is the concern to participate with others in a process in which *all of us together* can be made whole.

Would Tillich have agreed with my hypothesis? As I read him, he very nearly asserts it himself. He does so in a poignant passage in "Participation and Knowledge" where he distinguishes between level-one and level-two knowledge, as I have numbered them. He makes it clear that the healing "insight" into oneself that is a goal of the psychotherapeutic process belongs to the deeper, second level. He goes on to say, however, that this healing insight cannot happen when people confuse the two levels and conceive the healing as though it were the application of objective, level-one knowledge. As Tillich puts it,

> The meaning of depth psychology is completely misunderstood, if insight is interpreted as the knowledge and self-application of psychotherapeutic theories. . . . Insight is healing knowledge because it is the conscious participation in situations, processes, and strivings of present and past which have been covered, repressed, forgotten. Self-knowledge participates and becomes insight not in an externally remembered past, but [in] an internally reactivated one. Every analyst knows that scientific knowledge of the psychological processes involved makes reactivation, insight, and healing almost impossible. The difference of the cognitive levels is obvious. (MW 1:386)

It is significant that the healing Tillich describes here takes place in considerable measure at the middle cognitive level. We would expect the risk of confusing the situation and obstructing the healing to be even greater in the case of religion. For religion finds its home and "does its thing" at the deepest level.

If we do not involve ourselves at the level at which existential healing happens, we are not into religion. Yet, as I have argued,[10] when we are operating at that religious level, we have nothing to offer, nothing to share, except what has healed us. It is a matter of "one way"—one way to be saved or existentially healed—so far as what we can be "into" in a healing way in our own spiritual quest, or with other persons.

Of course, we do not have to relate to other religions or their adherents at the existential level, the level at which we are likely to feel this exclusivist impulse. As I have noted, it would be strikingly unusual for interfaith dialogue to take place at this deepest level.[11] However, if and insofar as we do relate to our religious "other" at this level—and insofar as we have not taken a vacation from religion!—this "one way" thing I have been talking about is likely to happen.

3. Why Contextual Exclusivism Belongs in Evangelical Theology

In the previous section I am not saying that, if we are Christian, for example, we must expect existential healing to happen only in the Christian religion. Categorical exclusivism of that kind is not characteristic either of Tillich or of the position I am proposing. As we have seen, Tillich is quite able to say that such healing happens elsewhere.[12] What he cannot do, at least on my analysis, is to give *personal and existential witness* to these other complexes of religious actuality *as healing*. What he *can* do is to give existential witness to what grasps and transforms him within the Christian tradition. And his theology is a way of doing that.[13]

---

[10]In the preceding chapter, on pp. 70-71.

[11]In the previous chapter, on pp. 65-66.

[12]In chap. 4, on p. 62; and see Tillich, "Missions and World History," 283-84; cf. ST 1:144; 3:220; Paul Tillich, *My Search for Absolutes* (New York: Simon and Schuster, 1967) 140-41.

[13]We even find some of this existential witness in Tillich's late essays on interreligious encounters, despite the fact that in these essays, Tillich "for the most part studiously avoids privileging one religion over another," as I say on p. 63 of the preceding chapter. In one account of his 1960 dialogues with Buddhists

It is in this way that Tillich provides for a missionary and evangelizing witness on the part of the Christian community. And Tillich clearly intends to provide for such a witness. He is explicit that missionary activity and evangelistic proclamation, along with education and practical apologetics (which is itself evangelistic), are ingredients in the "expanding functions" of the Christian church (ST 3:193-96).

To be sure, there is another side of Tillich's theology, even at this point, although I do not believe it will pose a problem for the good number of evangelicals who are inclusivists in attitude.[14] The other side of Tillich's theology at this point is the fact that he believes other religions have a missionary role in relation to the Christian community, as well as vice versa.[15]

In any case, the exclusivist-tending, "one-way-to-be-saved" quality that appears in the kinds of context I illustrated in the Buddhist-Christian dialogue in the previous chapter[16] is an important feature of religion—or of religion as a living whole when it has not "gone on vacation," I should say. To describe the attitude in which we are both aware of this feature of religion and ready to be a part of it, I have proposed the category of "contextual exclusivism." As noted, the adjective "contextual" indicates that exclusivism is not our baseline attitude; and the adjective also signals that we are able to leave it an open question whether, in other concrete contexts, our own religion may *not* be the available

---

in Japan, Tillich speaks of Christianity's commitment to salvation in history, and gently avows his conviction that Buddhism, which lacks this concern with history, does not appear to supply the necessary basis for transforming society, or for the democracy then being instituted in Japan. Tillich, *Christianity and the Encounter of World Religions* (1963) 72-75; (1994) 45-47; MW 5:316-17.

[14]Cf. Clark H. Pinnock, *A Wideness in God's Mercy: The Finality of Jesus Christ in a World of Religions* (Grand Rapids MI: Zondervan, 1992); and a book written by Pinnock's former student, John Sanders, *No Other Name: An Investigation into the Destiny of the Unevangelized* (Grand Rapids MI: Eerdmans, 1992).

[15]See Tillich, "Missions and World History," 288. Tillich's intention would be clearer here if the original title of this essay had been retained, namely, "The Theology of Missions." See n. 3 here above.

[16]On pp. 70-71, above.

vehicle of ultimate remedy or rescue, or of some measure of such remedy and rescue, in any case.

But can we realistically expect evangelicals to accept any view that says, as contextual exclusivism says, that it is *only in certain contexts* that the Christian message provides the "one way to salvation"? Yes, we can expect that. Most evangelicals of at least modest theological sophistication say the same thing in other words. That is, they give credence to the following two-sided doctrine: (a) when human beings proclaim the Christian message, they are able to give expression only to the "general" or "outward" call to faith; and (b) no regeneration and no conversion can take place *except in those contexts* in which the "special, inward, and effectual" call of the Spirit is present also, working through what the human agents in that context are doing.[17]

This two-sided doctrine is stated in such stark clarity by high Calvinism that we might take note of that position in order to make my point clear. According to such Calvinism, the most gifted evangelist could preach every night year after year to a room full of nonelect people, and nothing salvific would happen. The reason is that the Spirit would never work inwardly and effectually in the hearts of that group of hearers.[18]

I cite this high Calvinist idea in order to make my point vivid, however, and not because such Calvinism is characteristic of evangelicals generally. My point, which is embraced generally by theologically informed evangelicals, is that the Spirit's saving work is *only contextually* conjoined with the human witness to the Christian gospel. Of course, Christian preachers and teachers hope, expect, and believe that the Spirit is present and effective when they share the Christian message. But to claim this as a certainty is arrogant

---

[17]Cf. evangelical theologian Stanley J. Grenz's work, *Theology for the Community of God* (repr.: Grand Rapids MI: Eerdmanns, 2000) 413-14. (The first edition [Nashville: Broadman & Holman, 1994] has a different pagination.)

[18]See Calvin's distinction between general or outward, and special or inner calling. Only the inner can be effectual, and even that seems not to guarantee that one is elect. See John Calvin, *Institutes of the Christian Religion*, Library of Christian Classics 21, ed. John T. McNeill, trans. Ford Lewis Battles et al. (Philadelphia: Westminster Press, 1960) bk. 3, chap. 24, sect. 8, pp. 974-75.

presumption, simply on the grounds of sound evangelical theology itself.

Thus the conclusion follows: contextual exclusivism is not repugnant to, but is in fact required by, theologically literate evangelicalism.

4. The Connection with Liberation Theology

Up to a point, I am satisfied with the picture of contextual exclusivism that I draw in the preceding section. By Tillichian standards, however, there is at least one respect in which that picture does not go far enough. The picture as thus far drawn implies that the healing or fulfillment that religions offer has in all cases to do, mostly if not entirely, with the individual as individual. That limitation of the preceding section is appropriate in its place, because in the previous section I was relating Tillichian thought to evangelicalism, and evangelicals have a tendency to think of salvation in an individualistic way, if not also in an excessively otherworldly way as well. This is one of the points, again, at which Tillich is more biblical—in the sense of the Christian Bible—than evangelicalism.[19]

In order to bring out the more-than-merely-individual dimension of salvation, as Tillich and the Christian Bible see it, I want now to make a connection between Tillichian contextual exclusivism and liberation theology. That theology is acutely aware of the corporately social and concretely historical aspects of salvation within the Bible.

Making this connection with liberation theology may also have a secondary benefit. While a good number of nonevangelical Christians will find it a dubious recommendation of Tillich that his theology has any affinities at all with evangelicalism, many of these nonevangelicals likely will find it more appealing that there is also a connection to be made between Tillich and liberation theology.

The connection between Tillich and liberation theology is anything but farfetched. One link between the two is Tillich's concept of "kairos." What Tillich means by a kairos will be clearest if we

---

[19]See n. 3 in this chapter, p. 77 above.

take a paradigm example. The great kairos for Christians, as expressed in Jesus' proclamation in the gospels, is, "The time [*kairos*] is fulfilled, and the kingdom of God has come near; repent, and believe in the good news" (Mark 1:15 NRSV). In addition to this great kairos, Christians typically believe that other kairoi arise within the historical process, each standing under the judgment of the great kairos, and each drawing its power from that event, because, for Christians, this great kairos provides the center for all history, as we shall see in chapter 8 below.

In general, a kairos is an unusual moment in history in which eternity breaks into time, shaking it in a crisis, transforming it with uplifting power, demanding certain decisions, and "offering" to accomplish certain things in that situation that could not happen at another time. Tillich proclaimed a kairos in the early 1920s in Weimar Germany. He did this in the name of religious socialism, and under the criterion of the great Christian kairos. But in that situation, as he says, "a demonically distorted experience of *kairos*" won the day in National Socialism; and there ensued the destructive and self-destructive consequences that the demonic always brings in train (ST 3:371, cf. 369-72; MW 4:337).[20]

More than any other twentieth-century thinker, it was Tillich who made "kairos" a staple of theological discourse, both in his lifetime and since that time.[21] So far as the link with liberation theology is concerned, when Tillich first published his idea of kairos in 1922, he provided a virtual recipe for the liberation theologies that would arise after about 1970. [22]And these theologies have

---

[20]The MW reference is equivalent to Tillich, *The Protestant Era* (Chicago: University of Chicago Press, 1948) 45.

[21]The "kairos" entry in each of the following dictionairies mentions Tillich, and only Tillich, in defining the term: Van A. Harvey, *A Handbook of Theological Terms* (New York: Simon & Schuster, 1964); and Alan Richardson and John Bowden, eds., *Westminster Dictionary of Theology* (Philadelphia: Westminster, 1983).

[22]Tillich did this in remarks about the "absolute-revolutionary" interpretation of history. In the passage in question, he takes note of the different cognitive levels we have discussed. The passage begins with a reference to the great objective historians of the decades prior to 1922. For these scholars, he says, "history was an object of causal explanation or of exact descriptions, but it did not concern them existentially. It was not a place of actual decisions. . . . But

returned the compliment by making important use of the kairos idea.[23]

But what does all this have to do with contextual exclusivism? Liberation theologians are well known for urging that we cannot understand the saving or liberating work of the God of the Bible except as we exercise a "preferential option" for the poor and oppressed. When we take the standpoint of these marginalized people and involve ourselves existentially with their struggle for salvation or liberation, it becomes clear to us *in that existential location* that the divine work of liberation does not equally champion the virtues, values, and interests of all the parties in the situation, rich and poor alike, oppressor and oppressed alike. Rather, in the work that the biblical God does in this situation of oppression—in this kairos—*God takes one side against the other*. God takes the side of the poor and oppressed.[24]

This kind of one-sidedness is another example, in this case a more social-historical example, of the "one-way phenomenon" I have been talking about in my discussion of contextual exclusivism. In both cases, the inbreaking work of God takes shape, in this or in that concrete situation, as a single healing or liberating thrust. And for those existentially involved with it, that thrust has its judging and empowering force through one set of religious symbols. Here again we encounter the "one way to be saved" phenomenon.

Of course, if we stand back from the situation, it is conceivable that "other ways," other symbolisms, other religions, might also have served. While we are "on vacation from religion" in this way,

---

oppressed and ignorant people, and those few from the educated classes who identified themselves with the people, created the revolutionary-absolute interpretation of history" (MW 4:331; = Tillich, *Protestant Era*, 37).

[23]See Robert McAfee Brown, ed., *Kairos: Three Prophetic Challenges to the Church* (Grand Rapids MI: Eerdmans, 1990) as cited and discussed in idem, *Liberation Theology: An Introductory Guide* (Louisville KY: Westminster/John Knox Press, 1993) 100-105, 141-42.

[24]See Gustavo Gutiérrez, "Revelation and Theological Method" and "Truth and Theology," in *Gustavo Gutiérrez: Essential Writings*, ed. James B. Nickolof (Minneapolis: Fortress Press, 1996) 49-53 and 53-60; and see also Nickoloff's introduction, 12-13.

we may be as pluralistic as we wish! But if and insofar as we are involved at an existential level in this and then in that concrete situation, we shall again and again discover that actual healing and genuine liberation are making themselves effective, "here and now," in terms of just one complex of powerful symbols—that is, through one religion to the exclusion of others.

As noted, I propose the category of contextual exclusivism for the attitude that expects this kind of thing to happen, that recognizes it for what it is—a "one way to be saved" kind of thing—and that is ready to take part in it.[25]

5. Contextual Exclusivism as Prophetic

The difference between contextual and noncontextual exclusivism can be made clearer, I believe, if we take note of the way contextual exclusivism is prophetic. I intend the term "prophetic" in the sense of ancient Israel's great prophets, especially those of the eighth through the sixth centuries BCE. A prophet in this sense is not someone who engages in long-range, crystal-ball predictions. Rather, a prophet is one who speaks for Israel's God, pointing to what God is doing and/or demanding in certain events. Further, the events thus interpreted are taking place then and there within the unfolding life of Israel; or, at a minimum, they are potential future events that impinge directly upon the life of Israel then and there.[26]

Obviously Tillich's understanding of a kairos, which we previously discussed, is prophetic in the sense just explained. For example, he employs the term itself where he says that a kairos can "gain power in the prophetic word" that proclaims it—

---

[25]Another example of contextual exclusivism is my imaginary Buddhist-Christian scenario in chap. 3 above. There, in sect. 8, on pp. 70-71, I touched somewhat prematurely upon the category of contextual exclusivism, as I pointed out in that place.

[26]Cf. Bernhard W. Anderson assisted by Katheryn Pfisterer Darr, *Understanding the Old Testament*, abridged 4th ed. (Upper Saddle River NJ: Prentice-Hall, 1998) 223-25 (on the notion of the prophet's word as spokesman for God) and 227 (on the way that word points to and interprets specific events and situations in the history of Israel, and sometimes of Israel's neighbors).

although the presence of a kairos can neither be demonstrated nor forced (MW 4:339).[27]

As the two preceding paragraphs make clear, the prophetic word is a risky word. Tillich puts considerable emphasis upon this fact (ST 3:371). If we utter such a word, we may be mistaken. This is evident in the work of liberation theologians, for they sometimes seek to say how the inbreaking work of God is making itself felt, perhaps in a kairos, in such historical developments as the struggle of this or that particular group of poor for an end to their oppression.

The same risk will be present for us, also, if we speak in a contextually exclusivist way and say—to take a Christian example—that it is in "no other name" than that of Jesus that some particular audience "must be saved."[28] In such words we may not only prophesy falsely and be in error. We may also make a demonic claim in Tillich's sense of "demonic." That is, we may

---

[27]Equivalent to Tillich, *Protestant Era*, 48.

[28]The two quoted phrases come from Acts 4:12, one of the two chief proof texts for Christian exclusivists, the other being John 14:6. But the way I quote from the verse gives it only a *contextually* exclusivist sense. In fact, I do not believe the verse necessarily says any more than the following paraphrase: "There is no other salvation at hand for us, those of us here gathered, except in Jesus' name. Thus it is urgent: we must embrace it." I read it that way because of the imperative we read in the "b" part of the verse. The entire verse reads: "[a] There is salvation in no one else, [b] for there is no other name under heaven given among mortals by which we must be saved" (NRSV). If "b" said that it is only by Jesus' name that we *can* be saved, that might imply the universal proposition of the exclusivists. But instead of the indicative, we have this imperative: by Jesus' name alone "we *must* be saved." Because of this, I think that "b," *standing alone*, has only a contextually exclusivist meaning. I admit that the entire verse *sounds* exclusivist. (If it is exclusivist, nonexclusivists who want to square their positions with the New Testament as a whole will simply pit other texts against it.) However, the grammar indicates that "a" is a conclusion from "b," or, at a minimum, that "a" and "b" are very closely linked. I thus think "a" is only introducing and reinforcing "b," so that even when we take the verse as a whole, it affirms contextual exclusivism. Evangelical theologian Clark Pinnock, though he has made no comment on my argument above, argues on his own, different grounds, that the verse does not affirm exclusivism or "restrictivism." See Clark Pinnock, "Acts 4:12: No Other Name under Heaven," paper presented at a June 2002 conference in Edinburgh, a copy of which he shared with me in July 2002.

claim ultimacy for something that is only finite, as in the example of Nazism cited in the previous section of this chapter. Notwithstanding the risks, Tillich is surely right that it would be too great a loss if we sought to avoid all risk by flatly ruling out the validity, and indeed the imperativeness, of contextually exclusivist words of this prophetic kind.

We can sharpen the distinction between contextual and noncontextual exclusivism if we pursue a certain distinction within the Hebrew Bible that modern scholarship has made clear. I refer to the distinction between Israel's great prophets, on the one hand, and, on the other hand, those writers who compiled and edited the great "history" of "Israel in her land" that we find in Deuteronomy through 2 Kings.

These anonymous "Deuteronomistic historians" held to a certain generalization, or a certain universal proposition, namely, that in all cases in which the people of Israel obeyed God's laws, as given to Moses, they flourished, and when they turned aside from God's ways, they always suffered ruin. These writers directly state this proposition from time to time, and they quite clearly put their historical source material together so as to demonstrate the truth of their universal proposition—so far as their sources will allow them to do that.[29]

Although these historians' proposition is probably a generalization from what the prophets had been saying, I am interested in the difference, not the similarity, between the two. I am interested in the difference between the historians' *generalization* and the *contextual judgments* of the prophets. The reason I am interested in this difference is that, whereas the prophets' situational judgments are examples of contextual exclusivism, the historians' universal proposition is *analogous* to the universal proposition upheld by exclusivists.

The difference of the prophetic word is clear. The prophets typically dealt with such situations as the late eighth-century BCE invasion of Judah by an Assyrian army (Isaiah 10), or the series of victories won by the enlightened Cyrus the Great, who in about 540 BCE was soon to conquer Babylon. Making "situational calls"

---

[29] Anderson, *Understanding the Old Testament*, 166-67.

in specific contexts of this kind, the prophets proclaimed that God was active in these or in those events to judge or to save. God was *punishing* his people in the invasion. God was in the process of *liberating* his people from Babylonian bondage in what Cyrus was doing. These are contextual judgments.

My point here is not to take issue across the board with all generalizations, all universal propositions. The Deuteronomistic historians' theology of history handles very well the data they chose to illustrate it. More to the point, I shall later be proposing some hefty universal propositions myself. I shall do that when I make generalizations associated with reciprocal inclusivism. I shall affirm, for example, that when we find ourselves committed to our religion as our ultimate concern, there comes with that commitment the conviction, at least the implicit conviction, that the truth and salvation we detect in *every other religion* are included within (and judged by) the truth and salvation we find in our own faith.

Thus, rather than taking issue with all universal propositions as such, I am concerned to make these two points. First, in *addition* to our espousing universal propositions, I believe we need to be able to make the kinds of "contextual" judgments that the prophets made if we are to do justice to what religion is and does. And second, I believe we need to be able to adopt attitudes in some contexts that are *different from our usual, baseline attitude*. Though our baseline attitude may be inclusivist, for example, it is important that we are able also to experience and to adopt an exclusivist attitude when we are drawn deeply and existentially into certain situations. And I also believe we need to be able to adopt a pluralist stance when we deal with other religions in another context. This is notably the case when we take on the role of the scholarly interpreter of the facts concerning these other religions.

The contrast I have drawn here between the prophetic and the Deuteronomistic perspectives is not a perfect analogy to the contrast between contextual and noncontextual exclusivism. The Deuteronomistic writers were not exclusivists in our sense, and my analogy should not be taken to imply that the Deuteronomistic History provides a biblical basis for exclusivism. But for our purposes, the analogy is close. The point of comparison is the way the biblical historians *generalized* the prophets' situational judgments, transposing them into universal propositions about how things will always happen. That is what categorical exclusivists do.

One side of the contrast I have been discussing is brilliantly stated by Abraham Heschel. "The prophetic utterance," he says, "does not set forth a comprehensive law, but a single perspective. It is expressed *ad hoc*, often *ad hominem*, and must not be generalized."[30] As I hope I have made clear, what Heschel says applies also to the attitude and utterance of the contextual exclusivist.

6. Conclusion

Since I am recommending the contextual kind of exclusivism for all faiths—not just for evangelicals, and not just for Christians—I might conclude this chapter with an imaginary response that Tillich might make to people who think there is no room in his thought for exclusivism in any sense, and who prefer that it not be there.

Tillich might respond in the following way—which is fictional of course. "Let religious people give existential witness to what transforms them, and let them provide for that systematically in the way they interpret their own religion, and in the way they interpret and relate to other religions, as well. Don't try to restrict these people to levels of experience at which only something that is powerless to save can find its voice.

"And don't restrict me or my theology to those levels, either, not even if some of the things I say will have some kind of exclusivist implications."

---

[30]Abraham Heschel, *The Prophets* (New York and Evanston: Harper & Row, 1962) 23.

Chapter 6

Mysticism,
Multiple Religious Identities,
and Ethical Religion

The three things named in the title of this chapter—mysticism, multiple religious identities, and ethical religion—are objections that have been raised against what I propose in this book. That is, they are objections to what I propose here in part two, chapters 4–7, "Finding the Best Attitudes in Interreligious Encounters."

In the present chapter I not only deal with these three objections. I also provide some further development of the position I am proposing. This further development is provided as I place my position within the frame of Tillich's rich and illuminating typology of religion. This is the typology in which, most notably, he distinguishes sacramental, mystical, and ethical kinds of religion.

Tillich presented his typology to the public, with only nonessential changes, on at least nine occasions. One task I undertake in this chapter, especially in section 2, is to produce an epitome, and to some extent a synthesis, of these nine presentations. They extend from 1925 until the month of his death in 1965.[1]

---

[1] I list the nine texts in the order of their first publication or, in the case of lectures, their delivery. One reason the last text is important is that it tells us Tillich continued to hold to what he says in the first.
(1) Parts of Tillich's *Religionsphilosohie* (1925), in Paul Tillich, *What Is Religion?*, ed. James Luther Adams, trans. Adams and Charles W. Fox (New York: Harper & Row, 1969) 72-101.
(2) ST 1:211-25 (1951).
(3) The fourth chapter, "Types of Faith," in Tillich, *Dynamics of Faith* (New York, Evanston, and London: Harper & Row, 1957) 55-73; also in MW 5:256-65.
(4) Parts of the Matchette Lectures of April 1958 entitled "The Protestant Principle and the Encounter of World Religions," in Paul Tillich, *The Encounter of Religions and Quasi-Religions*, ed. Terence Thomas (Lampeter, Dyfed, Wales: Edwin Mellen Press, 1990) 21-31.
(5) At least the opening of the first of two unpublished lectures delivered in Chapel Hill NC, 3 and 4 October 1958, "The Present Encounter of World Religions," and "The Present Encounter of Religious and Secular Faiths," my own notes, taken while present at the lectures, in my files.

To be precise, the three objections with which I deal in this chapter pertain directly to *only one* of the proposals I have made thus far.[2] They attack the "level-three correlation." I developed that correlation in chapter 4[3] and made use of it in my discussion of contextual exclusivism in chapter 5. The correlation is the proposition that, when we encounter another religion at the third or most existential level, we usually feel ourselves drawn toward exclusivism—although it may well be that the exclusivism that is called for is only "contextual," that is, specifically for that particular situation.

The logical relations between the three objections and the case I am making are a little complex. On the one hand, much of what I say in the previous chapter depends upon the level-three correlation that these objections attack. That is to say, if we are *not* drawn toward exclusivism in a level-three interreligious encounter, we will not very often have occasion to adopt even a contextually exclusivist attitude.

Yet, on the other hand, my argument in the previous chapter is able substantially to carry its own weight. That is so because the argument is circular—in a healthy, not a vicious, way. The argument works as follows. If some of the points I make in chapter 5 are convincing—if I am persuasive in at least some of what I say about liberation theology, evangelical theologians, and the con-

---

(6)   A slide lecture of February 1959, "Art and Ultimate Reality," in which Tillich correlates five types of religion with as many stylistic elements in visual art, in Paul Tillich, *On Art and Architecture*, ed. John Dillenberger and Jane Dillenberger (New York: Crossroad, 1989) 139-57.

(7)   The 1962 Bampton Lectures (delivered in 1961), namely, Paul Tillich, *Christianity and the Encounter of the World Religions* (1963) 53-59; (1994) 33-37; MW 5:310-11.

(8)   ST 3:241-43 (1963), where Tillich distinguishes mysticism as an element in all religion from mysticism as one type of religion among others.

(9)   Some passages in Tillich's final lecture (12 October 1965), delivered some eleven days before his death, "The Significance of the History of Religions for the Systematic Theologian." This lecture is included as the appendix in the 1994 edition of item (7) above, that is, in *Christianity and the Encounter of World Religions* (1994) 64-66, 70-75, and is found also in MW 6:433-34, 436-39.

[2]In the next chapter, pp. 122-23, I list and summarize the five main proposals (four of them original) that I make in part two of this book.

[3]See sects. 7 and 9 of chap. 4.

textual exclusivism of the great Hebrew prophets, for example—
that fact tends to confirm the third-level correlation that my argument in that chapter "assumes." The reason is that the argument
"assumes" this correlation in a nonlinear, nondeductive way.

Nevertheless, the three objections pose some risk for my case.
Precisely how they pose this risk will be evident early in my discussion of the first objection.

I. Mystical Piety Is an Exception

When an encounter with another religion deepens for us and we
are put strongly in touch with the existential involvements that can
so powerfully move us, we are likely to feel an exclusivist impulse.
Or so I have argued.

But why should this level-three correlation be with exclusivism.[4] Why not with pluralism? Would we not expect that, the more
deeply we penetrate into the reality of the transcendent Source of
all, the more oneness we find—the more oneness with our religious others, and the more oneness between different religious
traditions?

In a superficial respect, this first objection to what I have
proposed is simply the popular and commonsense idea that "deep
down all religions are essentially the same—different paths leading
to the same goal." But in a profound way, this objection speaks for
the great Eastern mystical traditions, as in Hinduism and Buddhism; and this objection speaks also for a highly sophisticated
group of Western figures who can be grouped under the banner
of "the perennial philosophy."[5] One of these figures, Frithjof
Schuon, gives expression to the key idea in the title he puts on his
book, *The Transcendent Unity of Religions.*[6]

---

[4]This question was raised by John Thatamanil, now of Millsaps College, after
I delivered the original version of the ideas in this chapter at a meeting of the
American Academy of Religion Annual Meeting, Philadelphia, 19 November 1995.

[5]See the group discussed by Paul F. Knitter, *No Other Name?* 47-50, including
Aldous Huxley, Frithjof Schuon, and Huston Smith.

[6]Frithjof Schuon, *The Transcendent Unity of Religions*, rev. ed., trans. Peter
Townsend (New York: Harper & Row, 1975).

In answer to this first objection, my initial and basic reply is to
concede that, on Tillich's principles, there appears to be a small
exception to the level-three correlation I have proposed. In the
minority of human interreligious encounters in which the piety of
the person involved is predominantly *mystical*, we should expect
the tendency for such persons to be toward *pluralism*—rather than
toward exclusivism.

But why should we grant that exception? And if we do grant
it, how can we know that it is a small exception, as I have said it
is? And what is it about the nature of mystical religion, on the one
hand, and about the nature of other types of religion, on the other
hand, that ensures that the *main* level-three correlation continues
to be with exclusivism?

At this point the structure of correlations I have built up may
seem precarious. If we tend toward pluralism at the first or
detached cognitive level—as I conclude in chapter 4—and if the
mystical element in religion is actually quite widespread so that
we human beings also tend toward pluralism in much third-level
experience, as well, why should it be any different with our
middle-level interreligious encounters? In this way, as is obvious,
a good many of my conclusions could be weakened if not under-
mined.

2. Tillich's "Square-Shaped" Typology of Religions

In order to answer the questions just posed about mysticism and
its relation to other types of religion, I am going to have to deal at
some length with Tillich's "dynamic typology" of religion, as he
calls it.[7]

We begin by observing that, in considerable dependence upon
Rudolf Otto's classic work of 1917, *Das Heilige* (*The Idea of the
Holy*),[8] Tillich says that wherever we find the experience of the
Holy or the Sacred, there we find religion. And vice versa.
Wherever we find religion, there we find the experience of the

---

[7]Tillich, *Christianity and the Encounter of World Religions* (1963) 58; (1994) 36.
[8]Rudolf Otto, *The Idea of the Holy: An Inquiry into the Non-Rational Factor in the
Idea of the Divine and Its Relation to the Rational*, trans. John W. Harvey (New York:
Oxford University Press, 1943).

Holy, including its signature qualities, infinite mystery and a quality that combines the terrifying-shaking and the fascinating-attracting-uplifting.

In most of his discussions, Tillich treats sacramental religion as the original and basic type of the experience of the Holy.[9] For such religion, the focus is upon the finite realities in which the infinite or the Holy makes itself present for us. A sacramental reality in this sense can be an event, a person, an object, a certain practice, a word, or a sacred action or ritual. When Tillich says the sacramental type of religion is basic, he means that wherever the sacramental kind of experience is altogether absent, or no longer exists, we are not talking about religion—except in those cases in which the sacramental "pieces of reality," as Tillich calls them,[10] are only sleeping, and are at some point going to be revived or "recharged," as it were.

As these comments suggest, the sacred "punch" of a religion's sacramental realities can diminish as well as increase. In fact, this diminishment takes place in three different ways. I want now to discuss the three ways in which sacramental potency is diminished, the mystical, the ethical, and the secular-rational. These three ways will serve as a kind of "story line" for much of what I have to say.

We find in mysticism the gentlest of the three ways in which sacramental potency is diminished. The reason mysticism goes beyond the sacramental realities is that they are finite, and the mystic wants directly to reach the infinite or the absolute, the "one beyond the many." Mysticism does not typically attack or criticize sacramental things and actions. It accords them provisional respect. The rituals sometimes serve as purifying preparations for contemplation, and the concrete symbols—including divine figures—may serve as stepping stones for meditation that leads to union with the unconditional. Even so, the sacramental realities are denied their unconditional claim. They are devalued, made relative in favor of the absolute.

---

[9]Tillich presupposes a primitive "presacramental" stage of religion, as I shall shortly explain.

[10]Tillich, *Dynamics of Faith*, 59-60.

A second way in which sacramental potency is diminished derives from the prophetic-ethical element in the Holy. Typically this ethical kind of religion is roused to action by the fact that the sacramental realities, which are supposed to be *vehicles* of the Holy, are never satisfied merely to *be* vehicles. They want to be the real thing. Inveterately they claim to *be* the infinite and the Holy. And whenever their sacred fullness ceases to be convincing and unquestioned, they are ready to impose their finite perspectives and mandates in the name of the ultimate.

The claim of the finite to be unconditional in this way always brings destructive consequences. Tillich's name for this syndrome—the finite claim to ultimacy with its attendant tendency toward destructiveness—is "the demonic."

One striking feature of Tillich's idea of the demonic is the way he avoids blaming the ever-surging demonic tendency upon human individuals. His analysis is not moralistic. In his view, we exist because of our rootage in the energies of the infinite, the infinite looms up in our experience as the Holy, and within the Holy are both the divine—and the demonic!

Accordingly, much of the plot of the unfolding history of religions can be understood as an interplay between the divine and the demonic. At first these two are mixed, then they begin to be distinguished, and, as the differences are heightened, a struggle between them ensues. The struggle vectors toward an "endpoint" or *Zielpunkt*. The full realization of this endpoint or goal is beyond history, but it is nevertheless very effective within history. To the extent that this endpoint is reached in the development of the various religions, the divine *eliminates* the demonic—or rather, as Tillich proceeds to correct himself, the divine *integrates* the demonic into itself.[11] A bit later, we shall see how Tillich also conceives this telos of history in more positive terms as a union of the differing types of religion.

In any case, demonry does arise, and ethical-prophetic religion accosts the sanctified injustices that accumulate. This is done in the name of justice, but it is *divine* justice that is invoked, for ethical religion is *religion*; it is not just ethics. Often the demand for justice

---

[11]Tillich, *What Is Religion?*, 88; cf. GW 1:340.

becomes real as law. And it is, of course, understood as *religious* law, God's law.

Nevertheless—and this is important—the prophetic onslaught runs in the direction of secularizing things, at least in the long run. This is the case because, as sacred injustices are rebuked and moral grotesqueries are purged, *holiness* is dissipated.

The absolute demand of the right and the just are elements of the Holy on its divine side. But sacred realities are not usually ready to reform or to be reformed. Thus they are swept away or neutralized along with everything else that offends justice. Tillich's favorite example at this point is the way the Hebrew prophets declared that the God of Israel would destroy his own people—the chosen, the holy, the "sacramental" nation—because of its injustice (ST 1:227-28).

Thus far I have described a "triangle," as it were, a three-cornered struggle that involves mystical, ethical, and sacramental religion. In order to move forward—and in order now to deal with the third of the three ways in which sacramental "clout" is diminished—I suggest we envision a square, and not merely the triangle just described.

Tillich himself uses a "typological square" to explain his views. I follow him, although somewhat loosely.[12] The typological square I propose rests upon one of its corners so that it is rather like a baseball diamond. The corner that grounds everything, "home plate," is the sacramental basis of all religion. At "third base" is the mystical element, while at "first base" we have the prophetic-ethical element.

In the top corner, at "second base," we locate a factor that Tillich always brings onto the playing field when he presents his typology of religions. This factor is the rational-secular. "The secular is the rational," Tillich says, "and the rational must judge

---

[12]In his Chapel Hill lecture, "The Present Encounter of World Religions" (see item 5, n. 1 above), three of the corners of Tillich's typological square are the same as mine, namely, sacramental, mystical, and ethical. But whereas the upper corner of his square is the tendency for all the types to converge, my square describes this convergent tendency in another way. This allows me to use the upper corner for something else. I am about to explain what I mean by that.

the irrationality of the Holy. It must judge its demonization." And, again, "secularization is the third and most radical form of de-demonization."[13] He means it is the third form in addition to the mystical and the ethical-prophetic forms of de-demonization.

When the upper corner of our diamond does its rationalizing-secularizing work, it liberates our rational capacities. It does this in us both as individuals and as cultures. Thus we are likely to become "autonomous." And we often do.

This is not pure joy, however. Our finite autonomy is a condition in which we are tempted to forget the unconditional, to trivialize the infinite, and to make our finite-rational cultures and selves the All. When we do that, our lives are emptied of their substance, and—rid of their depth and robbed of their passion—they are ripe for the demonic onslaught of some new "passionate intensity," that is, some new and ghastly outbreak of the Holy as demonic.

Although my discussion has dwelt mostly upon conflicts and tensions, there are attractions as well conflicts among the religious types. The reason for this is that, despite their rivalries, each of the four corners needs the others in order for there to be a square. In concrete terms, that means no actual religion could live or move or exist without the presence within it of at least *some of each* of the "type-determining elements,"[14] the sacramental, the mystical, and the ethical. Thus, when we correctly identify a particular instance of religion in action as this or that type of religion, it only means that one of these type-determining elements is predominant in that particular outcropping of religion. All the elements are present, at least in some degree.

3. The Longitudinal Dynamics of the Typology

Thus far I have spoken mostly of what we might call "cross-field" conflicts and attractions. These cross-field polarities are probably the larger part of the dynamism that Tillich espies in his dynamic typology.

---

[13]Tillich, "The Significance of the History of Religions," 73-74.
[14]Tillich, *Christianity and the Encounter of World Religions* (1963) 57; (1994) 36.

But there is more. The attractions between the typological poles has a "longitudinal" as well as a cross-field dimension. That is to say, the entire square or diamond is caught up in an overarching drive toward something Tillich calls "the inner aim of the history of religions," or "theonomy."[15]

In order to visualize this longitudinal thrust, I suggest we "spin" our square upon its point—but for only half a turn, only far enough that we see the square "from its side" as a thin straight line. This done, we can imagine that the longitudinal drive is constantly moving the entire diamond "forward" through time, or from left to right. An alternative image is to see our square as a four-cornered kite that is driven by the wind from left to right.

More important than the visual image, however, is the fact that the telos *toward* which this longitudinal drive presses is "the religion of the concrete spirit." This theonomous goal involves a synthesis of all three of the type-determining elements that are present in the Holy. And the union includes our fourth corner, the secular-rational, as well!

This point can be documented from something Tillich says in his final lecture before his death. Although the unifying telos that is the inner aim of the entire history of religions is never fully reached, Tillich says, "I believe that there is no higher expression of what I call the synthesis of these three elements than in Paul's doctrine of the Spirit." He speaks of the three type-determining elements that belong to the Holy. But he then proceeds to add the fourth factor, the rational-secular. In the Pauline religion of the Spirit, he says, "we have the ecstasy and the rational elements, united."[16]

Corresponding to this endpoint, Tillich conceives also a "point of departure."[17] He says the relation between the two points is not chronological. Rather, the points are ideal. They are constructs, and the concrete reality of our experience is "between" them. However, just as Paul's religion of the Spirit *approximates* the "endpoint," it appears to be the case—though Tillich does not say this explicit-

---

[15]Tillich, "The Significance of the History of Religions," 74.
[16]Tillich, "The Significance of the History of Religions," 72.
[17]Tillich, *What Is Religion?*, 88-89.

ly—that the presacramental stage of religion *approximates* the "point of departure."

I think this presacramental stage of religion is integral to Tillich's dialectical grasp of the history of religions, and I doubt we can feel the force of his career-long thought on this subject without being aware of it. Perhaps there is an analogy to the way Engels thought Marx's dialectic was not complete without presupposing the stage of "primitive communism."[18]

Tillich describes this presacramental stage in the following vivid passage. When Tillich speaks of "form" in the passage, he is thinking of the rationally structured and intelligibly graspable aspect of reality, as in the dialectics of ground, form, and act (ST 3:284).

> Through the antidemonic influence of form the original undiffer-entiatedness [i.e., the mix of demonic and divine in the Holy in the presacramental situation] bifurcates into the polarity of two basic attitudes, one of which we shall call the sacramental and the other the theocratic tendency [or "prophetic-ethical" tendency in Tillich's latter language]. The sacramental attitude is seized by the criticism that form brings to bear, insofar as the sacramental attitude is no longer able to intuit the Holy undifferentiatedly in everything real, but instead considers [only] particular realities and forms as bearers of the Holy import. Precisely in this way these things and actions receive a sacramental quality.[19]

According to this passage, sacramental religion recognizes *only certain* things and actions as sacramental. This represents a change and a purification from the presacramental stage. In the earlier stage, *mana* is everywhere and *any thing, any action,* is apt to burst into flame with the sizzling presence of the Holy—even irrational and destructive things such as child sacrifice (cf. ST 1:222). The distinguishing of the divine from the demonic has now made its first clear step!

---

[18]See the famous footnote Engels adds at the beginning of *The Communist Manifesto.*

[19]Tillich, *What Is Religion?*, 88-89. In addition to my bracketed insertions, I have altered the published translation slightly to conform it to my reading of GW 1:340.

4. Why Mysticism Tends Pluralistic and Is Also a Minority Phenomenon

On the basis now of the typological theory I have explained, I hope in this section to achieve two ends. I hope to clarify why mystical piety, when it gets involved in a third-level interreligious encounter, tends toward a pluralistic attitude. And I hope also to say why that is a minority phenomenon, with the result that most religion tends toward exclusivism in such depth encounters.

(1) In one place Tillich provides a graphic description of the mystical tendency to go ecstatically beyond all finite forms in order to grasp the underlying ground of being and meaning. He writes: "In ecstasy, in the going beyond all forms of consciousness, or in submersion or absorption, in the sinking back into the ground of consciousness, mysticism finds its fulfillment."[20]

It is transparent here, especially in Tillich's language about "sinking back into the ground," that if we are strongly mystical in our piety and become involved in an interreligious encounter, we will instinctively press through the differences between ourselves and our religious "other" so as to find some underlying sameness or oneness. And it is almost axiomatic that we will "settle back into" or "luxuriate in" the oneness that we find at this level of depth. That is what it means that we relativize the finite in favor of the absolute. The mystical tendency to "reach beyond the particular" dulls the sharp edges of every difference that would separate us from our "other."

In a contrast between Buddhism and Christianity that I attempt in chapter 8 below, I try to make clear some of the East-West differences Tillich sees at this point, differences that underlie his contrast between historical and nonhistorical religions. I need to make one point here that I do not make in chapter 8, however. Tillich speaks of "mysticism" in two senses (ST 3:241-43). In a first sense, mysticism is simply the union of the finite with the infinite. In this sense, it is the core of all living religion, East and West.

---

[20]Tillich, *What Is Religion?*, 90.

But what is this finite-infinite union like? Is it a quiet sinking back, or a dynamic driving forward? Is it like stretching out in a hot bath, or like trying to unharness one's self from a parachute after hitting the ground in a windstorm? As I tried to make clear in chapters 2 and 3, Tillich has a highly dialectical, Western, Nicolas-of-Cusa-type understanding of the way the finite and the infinite are united. The infinite is constantly and dynamically positing itself and surpassing itself *within our finite reality*, and that means in and through the novelties of our history, with all the individual identities and personal attachments that pertain thereto—although Tillich also acknowledges the quieter union of finite and infinite as well, especially when he speaks of the ultimate as *ground* of being.

Now we look at Tillich's second sense of "mysticism." This is the sense I am using in most of the present discussion. In this sense, mysticism is one type of religion in contrast to other types. In the present instance, it contrasts especially with the ethical type of religion. The mystical type responds more to the holiness of the *is*, whereas the ethical type responds more to the holiness of the *ought to be*. Tillich seeks in his own position to achieve and provide for a union of the two types, the mystical and the ethical. Thus he criticizes both, insofar as either might "go it alone." However, there is one important sense in which his criticism of the mystical type cuts deeper. The ethical type tends toward making life secular, and that is bad. But this ethical drive is also a drive toward the rational. And that is good. Further, both the rational and the secular belong to the goal or endpoint toward which all human religious experience moves.

Thus, when mysticism "backs away" from, or takes a vacation from, historical and ethical engagements—scorning them so far as finding in them anything of *ultimate worth* is concerned—mysticism disconnects itself from the infinite in its dynamic mode, and "bails out" of the historical process. Whatever the divine infinite is up to in that process, mysticism is not interested, that is, not ultimately interested. This is the meaning behind Tillich's remark, quoted above, that the mystic "sinks back into the ground," at least as I read that statement.

Among the differences that are swallowed up in the mystic's experience are, of course, any differences of value or validity that might try to present themselves. The mystical tendency, I conclude, is strongly disposed in the direction of pluralism, that is, toward the recognition of equal value and validity, or least indifferent value and validity, among religions.

(2) Even if someone were inclined to judge the mystical way superior to other types of religious experience, I doubt that such a person would judge the mystical to be the *majority form* of faith.[21] I submit that the religious life of the large majority of religious people is oriented pivotally to the specific, concrete symbolisms of the religion in which they are involved.

As we have seen, that is what it means to be sacramentally religious. If sacramental religion is thus the majority form, the following is the case in most religion on this planet. People find that the sacramental objects and actions of their own tradition speak to them, whereas the corresponding accoutrements of other traditions are "excluded": they are excluded at least in the sense that they do not speak to these people in this profound way.

Of course it is then a second question, as we saw in chapter 4, whether the exclusivist impulse or tendency that asserts itself in this manner will move beyond an *inability to affirm* saving truth in other religions to the point at which it *denies* that other faiths have such truth. Only the second of these two is exclusivism proper.

But, if my argument is sound, the tendency in that exclusivist direction is present in the majority of deep, existential religious experiences. And that is all I assert when I propose that there is a correlation between level-three experience and an exclusivist attitude.

Although I have not fully discussed prophetic-ethical religion in this section, I do examine it in section 5, immediately below. For this phase of my argument, however, I do not need to deal with it. Whatever is the case with ethical religion, if the majority of the religious experiences of humankind are sacramental, and if sacra-

---

[21]Frithjof Schuon believes conventional exoterics, as he calls them, vastly outnumber the esoteric mystics. See Huston Smith's introduction in Schuon, *The Transcendent Unity of Religions*, ix-xxvi.

mental piety—in its deepest moments—tends toward exclusivism, then the main correlation of third-level religion with exclusivism stands, and mysticism's tendency toward pluralism ranks as the minority exception.

5. Multiple Religious Identities

Against the level-three correlation I have just restated it has been objected that some people have multiple religious identities. The argument is quite straightforward. How could there be any such thing as a multiple religious identity if, in our deepest experiences, our identity takes shape around one religion to the exclusion of others? But some people *do* confess more than one religious identity. Hence my level-three correlation must be mistaken—at least in the case of these individuals.[22]

I have implicitly answered this objection, at least in part. At a minimum, *some* of those who have more than one religious identity will be predominantly mystical in their piety. As I have conceded, these people will be aware of pluralistic tendencies at the deeper level at which their identities have been formed. Thus, for any multiple-identity people who are mystics, there is no conflict with the position I am proposing.[23]

Further, inasmuch as my third-level correlation is a general rule that admits of exceptions, *a fallback position* is already implicit in what I have said. That position would be to consider multiple-identity people, whether they happen to be mystics or not, as exceptions to the main level-three correlation.

I would prefer, however, not to fall back upon the position just stated. At a minimum, I would like to account for these exceptions on Tillichian principles and not treat them simply as unexplained anomalies. In addition, I would also like to be assured that these

---

[22]I am indebted to A. Durwood Foster of the Pacific School of Religion for raising this objection. He did so in 1995 after I presented some of the ideas in this chapter for the first time.

[23]See John Thatamanil's interpretation of his own dual religious identity as both a Christian and an Advaitic Hindu. John J. Thatamanil, "Managing Multiple Religious and Scholarly Identities," *Journal of the American Academy of Religion* 68 (December 2000): 791-803; cf. 797-801.

multiple-identity persons really are small in number. If the exceptions outnumber the nonexceptions, a general rule is not much of a rule!

Accordingly, I seek to accomplish two things in the remainder of this section, namely, to account for multiple identities on Tillichian grounds, and to make it convincing that genuine multiple identities are few in number. In order to do so I employ two analogies.

(1) My first analogy is that of "the switch hitter." *Within* each batting stance, both in the left-handed position and in the right-handed position, so to speak, the Tillichian principles apply. Here we may take as an example a person who immerses herself so deeply and extensively in Buddhism that, according to her confession of faith, she is now Buddhist as well as Christian.[24] She practices some branch of the Buddhist tradition in addition to maintaining the practice of some recognizable species of Christian faith.

To interpret such a case in Tillichian terms we simply say that the Christian Buddhist has the rare and hard-won capacity to switch back and forth between two different religious orientations.

This is not to say that the person's life will be sliced up without remainder into mutually exclusive spans of time, half Buddhist and half Christian, or whatever the ratio might be. It is only to say that a significant number of this person's moments—notably, most of her deeper or level-three experiences—will be *either* Christian *or* Buddhist moments, but not both.

For example, there might be Christian moments in which this person experiences love in the sense of attachments to other persons, ultimate attachments that are to be fulfilled in the Kingdom of God, whereas in other moments, all such attachments would be felt as preultimate, things to be transcended in the experience of Nirvana. I add that the distinctiveness of these Christian moments remains, in this particular Christian-Buddhist case, even if the Kingdom of God is experienced in symbolic terms. Or that would

---

[24]In the interest of gender equality, I use a woman as my example here and a man in the next chapter, where I speak of an "activist."

be the case so long as it was a *kingdom* that was effective as the symbol, namely, a social, political, and interpersonal reality.[25]

But what if a person with a multiple religious identity manages *simultaneously* to practice two or more religions, even in this person's deeper mindset or orientation, and in his or her sense of what one most truly is?

To deal with such cases, I first submit that they are highly unusual, and that they belong in a group of exceptions that is so small as to pose no problem for my general rule. If it is then objected that belonging simultaneously *and existentially* to two religions is something that is really quite widespread, I would reply with my second analogy. It is designed to show that, although many people may have multiple identies in some very weak sense, most of these would-be multiple identities are not really multiple after all.

(2) Here I invoke my second analogy, that of a "team approach." To the extent that our religious adept practices two or more faiths simultaneously, and does so without pathological personal fragmentation, I believe the religious traditions involved—at least in nearly all circumstances—are showing us that they are *capable of a team approach.*

The kind of thing I have in mind is easier to envision if we view it on a sociocultural scale. And it is also in this sociocultural context that we are able not merely to envision this kind of thing, but also to *account for* the overwhelming majority of would-be multiple identities.

I point to the relation between Confucianism and Taoism in much Chinese history, and to the relation between Shinto and Buddhism in much Japanese culture. These religious traditions have long been experienced as sufficiently complementary that they can operate "as a team." There is even some division of labor between them as they tend to deal with differing existential needs within their respective populations—which are, for the most part, the same people.

---

[25]Cf. Tillich, *Christianity and the Encounter of World Religions* (1963) 63-66; (1994) 39-41; MW 5:313-14.

Within these sociocultural settings, and within the persons situated there, a patterned ensemble of elements from the two different traditions operates *like one religion*. Within the sphere of that "one religion," a team-religion, the exclusivist tendencies I have remarked put in their appearance. That is, people find that alien symbolisms from *outside* that "one religion" do not avail— although, as I have noted, this one religion is two religions so far as its historical traditions and much of its institutionalized infrastructure are concerned.

This broad sociocultural description, so it would appear, accounts for the vast majority of would-be cases of multiple religious identity. It indicates that, in the sense that is relevant to my argument, these people have only one religious identity.

One difference between the sociocultural and the personal level helps to make what I am saying more concrete. Once the teamed-up ensemble of elements is internalized in the young person or adult, it operates in good measure from a location "inside" that individual. By contrast, in the Chinese and Japanese examples I cited, I focused upon the way the ensemble of religious elements operates "outside" people, or from out of their ambient culture.

6. Ethical Parity and Pluralism

At their best, religions have enough of the ethical element in them to draw their adherents into one embracing, *rational* community of righteousness, justice, and concern for all. And I emphasize the word "rational" in the preceding sentence for reasons that will become apparent. If we find different religions doing a good job in their ethical missions within their respective societies, we may be prompted toward a pluralistic conclusion. Or we may not. It depends upon other factors.

In either case, however, that kind of comparative evaluation is an exercise we carry out primarily at level one, or perhaps at both levels one and two. It involves dispassionate, detached assessment of these other faiths, perhaps combined with some degree of understanding empathy with them.

In order to see what things look like at level three, however— that is, from a perspective that is *within* our involvement with a concrete religion—we might imagine a project in which we are engaged. It takes place, we shall say, in a society that is multireligious; and we are involved in a joint or interreligious project. This fictional project is one in which several of us from different religious traditions work together for justice, for example, in an interfaith soup kitchen.

In such a setting, we could hardly fail to experience considerable empathy with other faiths. We shall probably find that the values and transforming power of our own religion are present also in the different faiths of the other people involved in the project. As that fact signals, we would be hard pressed to avoid coming to at least a weak kind of inclusivistic view.

Is it possible that we shall also experience a deeper commonality with these other people, a religious commonality? In one kind of situation this could happen, and it could also bring pluralistic implications with it. But, on Tillich's principles, this is something that would take place only in times of relative "theonomy" or religious fullness. Though we humans experience foretastes of that "eschatological" fullness, and though our life is always moving toward it, the spans of time that are strongly marked by it are rare. I shall accordingly put this possibility aside. I do so wistfully, but with a determination to look at the facts.

What we actually have, then, is situations in which, even when our religion impels us into social justice concerns, and even when this brings us together in common cause with those of other faiths, it is most likely that *what we experience in common* with these others will be far more secular-ethical than it will be religious-ethical.

This point becomes especially convincing, at least to me, in the light of what Tillich says about the ethical type of religion. As it gathers itself into a rationally worked-out pattern of action, it tends toward the secular—absent some inbreak or upsurge of theonomy, a possibility that I have set aside.

The result is something like this. When we engage in the same outward, ethically driven behaviors as those of other faiths, the *religious meaning* of what we are doing will not be the same, and our *religious identities* will be different. Caring for others as Christ loved us, living the Muslim "way," and expressing Buddhist compassion are not the same thing, even though our conduct—especially when we engage in it jointly with those of other faiths—may *look* the same to the outside observer.

So long as differences of this kind remain important to each of the religious parties, they are not likely to find that different religions are equal or indifferent in value and validity, even if these religions appear to be on a par in the matter of eliciting moral behavior.

7. Conclusion

The upshot of this chapter can be stated simply and quickly. In order to give the position I am developing a more thickly described chracter, this chapter has set it within the frame of Tillich's lively and illuminating typology of religion. With this Tillichian theory serving also as part of our base, and having accounted for the phenomenon of multiple religious identities, we were able to conclude that the main third-level correlation I have proposed stands.

However, that correlation allows for a relatively small exception in the case of those whose faith is predominantly mystical. For the mystics, even the deepest experiences of interreligious encounter—especially the deepest experiences!—will have a pluralistic ring. But for those whose faith is predominantly sacramental or ethical, the normal tendency at this deep level will be exclusivistic, although the exclusivism that is called for may be of quite a contextual kind, and feeling an exclusivist tendency does not make one exclusivist.

Chapter 7

Reciprocal Inclusivism

My primary concern in this chapter is to explain and recommend a nuanced form of inclusivism that I call "reciprocal inclusivism." I believe this neologism best describes the interreligious attitude that is both warranted and called for by Tillich's thought. It was probably also Tillich's own interreligious attitude, but I do not pursue that issue. My concern in this book is not biographical. In any case, my recommending this attitude is done both on the basis of Tillich's thought and as a matter of personal conviction.

But I need to be a bit more specific about what I am recommending. I recommend this attitude as the most adequate attitude *overall* for interreligious encounters.[1] I support it as the most apt and auspicious baseline attitude, or the most promising characteristic perspective for us to maintain in our dealings with other faiths.[2]

In addition to recommending something as a baseline attitude in this chapter, I have of course already recommended two "contextual" attitudes. In chapters 4 and 5, respectively, I argue that, depending upon the nature and depth of the particular interreligious encounter in question, we do well to be ready and able to adopt either a contextually pluralist, or a contextually exclusivist, stance. For example, contextual pluralism would be appropriate in doing comparative religious study, whereas contextual exclusivism may be called for in that rare interreligious encounter in which we

---

[1] See the introduction to chap. 4 for the broad range of experiences that count as "interreligious encounters" in the sense I have in mind.

[2] As explained in my introduction to this book, when I use such expressions as "our own faith," or one's own religion," I refer to whatever religion a reader is most familiar with. I refer to the faith that supplies this reader with his or her clearest ideas of what other religions are like. In this way, even people who do not consider themselves religious are included when I speak of "our own religion" and the like. By the same token, when I speak of "another religion," or "other religions," I mean religions other than the one the reader belongs to, or is most familiar with, as the case may be.

are genuinely invited to give existential witness to what most deeply grasps us, and most profoundly shapes who we are.[3]

In sum, I believe we are best advised to be reciprocal inclusivists in our baseline attitude, and to be contextual pluralists and contextual exclusivists—all three. Only in that way, it seems to me, do we have any prospect of doing justice to the richness of the role of religion in human life, and of doing justice to the imperatives of our own religion as well.

I. The Dynamics of All Religious Experience

In order to understand what a Tillichian kind of reciprocal inclusivist attitude might be, a good place to begin is with the dynamics to be found in every religious experience or encounter, as Tillich sees the matter.

In Tillich's understanding of the dynamics of any interreligious encounter, two opposite tendencies or "thrusts" are at work. There is both a "stay-at-home" and a "move-onward" or a "moving-beyond" tendency, as I might characterize them.

Actually, these opposed drives are present in the human situation as such, and not simply in religious or interreligious experience. But that means they are certainly present also in the middle-level interreligious encounters. We are especially interested in this middle level because, as we saw in chapter 4, inclusivism is correlated with that level of encounter.

What accounts for the conflicted situation that Tillich finds in every religious experience? What is it, on the one hand, that can lure us beyond our simply staying at home and reiterating the formulas of our familiar faith? What is this *moving-beyond* tendency? And, on the other hand, what is it that nevertheless restrains

---

[3]When I speak of a "rare encounter," I mean that the *interreligious* occasions upon which existential witness is appropriate are rare. I certainly do not mean that the occasions for existential witness are rare. They are quite frequent, not only for religious leaders but also for devout laypersons. But not many of these occasions are *inter*religious. They are typically *intra*religious, as in worship, or in a religious instruction class. Even evangelization and mission are not normally interreligious undertakings.

us from simply "moving into the lodgings" of some other faith? What is this *stay-at-home* tendency?

Tillich's answer to these questions is to point to the tension between ultimacy and concreteness. This tension, he says, is integral both to the idea of God and to our experience of ultimate concern. That is to say, it is integral to our being religious. On the one hand, if we are to be ultimately concerned with something, it "must transcend every preliminary finite and concrete concern. It must transcend the entire realm of finitude." Here we see the drive toward ultimacy. We might call it "the pull of the infinite."

On the other hand, the drive toward concreteness is also present. "[I]t is impossible to be concerned about something which cannot be encountered concretely," Tillich writes, "be it in the realm of reality or in the realm of imagination. Universals can become matters of ultimate concern only through their power of representing concrete experiences" (ST 1:211; cf. 214, 215, 22).

This drive toward concreteness is as strong as we are finite. In fact, this drive more or less *is* our finitude. One thing it means is that we cannot "have" God, that is, we cannot experience the presence and power of the divine, except in symbols.[4] Religious symbols participate in and point to the infinite or the unconditional. Nevertheless, they themselves are conditioned and finite. Furthermore, during any one period of time we are "stuck" with the religious symbols that are powerful for us. We cannot interchange these symbols at will, and their power to mediate the divine to us may wax or wane. Their power grows or dies with the liveliness of the particular religion that shapes and partly determines what we most deeply are.[5]

In the light of what Tillich says about these two opposed drives and the need to include them both, we are encouraged to think that the ideal will be some kind of balance between them. And that, in turn, suggests that inclusivism of some kind will be the best attitude to have in interreligious encounters, since inclusivism includes both a "staying at home" with one's own faith and a

---

[4]See pp. 40-42, above.

[5]Tillich's doctrine of the religious symbol is explained in numerous places. See ST 1:238-41, and chaps. 13, 22, and 24 in MW vol. 4.

"being drawn beyond it" in appreciation for other faiths. But what kind of inclusivism might suffice?

2. What Is Reciprocal Inclusivism?

Religious attitudes are not easy to explain. To make the present explanation of reciprocal inclusivism as clear and concrete as possible, I shall do something unusual throughout most of this section. I will make use of a fictional Christian-Muslim encounter, and I will put some of the imagined exchanges in the first person.

Despite my use of the first person in this section, what I say is not confessionally Christian. The invented encounter is only a rhetorical example. It is intended to represent the dynamics of encounter between *any* two religions. We could substitute for the Christian or the Muslim an adherent of any faith. And further, we could let any of the parties in the encounter, no matter what their religion, be the one who speaks in the first person.

That said, I may be free to speak as follows.

Because we Christians generally are not shaped or partly determined by your religion, my Muslim friend, the transforming, saving truth of your faith touches us in only a limited way, if it does so at all. Furthermore, when we do find ourselves able to sense some of the transforming power in your religion, it is usually only to the extent that we participate empathetically in the things in your religion that are analogous to this or that potent Christian symbol or theme.

Thus, as an inclusivist Christian, I confess that I experience the transforming or saving truth of Islam—insofar as I do experience it—as not only included within, but as also judged by, the saving truth of my Christian faith. This is a consequence of my finitude, or of my being in the grip of the drive toward concreteness, the stay-at-home side of my being.

In addition to this drive or tendency toward the concrete, however, the opposite tendency is in me also, that is, the drive toward ultimacy. To whatever extent I am in the grip of this drive, I am enabled to worship the God who is really God rather than some concrete idol, for I am constrained by what we might call "the Anselmic principle." By the force of this principle I am kept aware that the divine reality is greater than the manner in which

I am able to conceive it or experience it. As St. Anselm phrased this, God is "that, than which nothing greater can be conceived."[6]

Interrupting this Muslim-Christian dialogue, I should like to point out that, up to this paragraph, we are talking about generic inclusivism. Inclusivism is our saying that the saving truth of other faiths is included within our own, but is judged thereby, as well. In the next paragraph, when the fictional encounter resumes, we move beyond mere inclusivism to reciprocal inclusivism.

In keeping with the Anselmic principle, I am drawn, not only to inclusivism, but to "reciprocal inclusivism." This is the attitude in which I acknowledge the following proposition, and I hope you will too, my Muslim friend. Just as I view Islam's saving truth as included within and judged by the truth of Christianity, I expect you to view the saving truth in Christianity as included within your truth, and as judged by your truth.

But that is only part of what we mean by reciprocal inclusivism. If I am responding in this encounter in a Tillichian manner, I will not only *expect* you to think that my truth is included within and judged by yours. I will actually *approve* of the fact that you do so. I thus encourage and support you in your Muslim way, and I expect and hope that you will likewise encourage and support me in my Christian life.[7] *And* I do so even when your faith constrains you to criticize and judge mine. One good reason why I am motivated to do this rather strange-sounding thing is that I want you to be faithful to whatever divine revelation has reached you— up until now.

And one more point. Just to make a clean breast of it, let me add that I cannot help but hope that at least some of the saving

---

[6]Anselm, *Proslogium*, chap. 3, in St. Anselm, *Proslogium; Monologium; An Appendix on Behalf of the Fool by Gaunilon; and Cur Deus Homo*, trans. Sidney Norton Deane (La Salle IL: Open Court, 1961) 8.

[7]In order not to complicate the situation I am describing, I ignore the negative or destructive elements that are present in every actual religion. I bring into consideration only the wholesome elements that deserve to be affirmed. In a full accounting, I would need to identify demonic tendencies in both faiths and say something about how they should be rejected and resisted. In terms of Tillich's thought (see pp. 98-99, 102, above), I speak only of the divine and ignore the demonic ingredient in the Holy that is manifest in the two religions.

truth of my faith, preferably all of it, will somehow be opened up or revealed for you, and that some of that might happen in the course of this encounter in which we are involved. And I fully expect you to have the same hope.

I conclude now, speaking from a position outside the fictional encounter.

To be an inclusivist is to affirm something about other faiths in this pattern: their saving truth is included in, but also judged by the saving truth in my religion. To be a reciprocal inclusivist is to go beyond that affirmation in such a way that we *expect* that the representatives of other faiths will have the same inclusivist attitude toward our faith, and also—here is the trademark feature—to *approve* the fact that these other parties adopt an inclusivist attitude toward our faith, and to approve this fact even when the other parties' inclusivism entails their judging our faith.

3. Is the Inclusiveness Fully Symmetrical? Can We *Experience* Pluralism?

An important question arises at this point. Is the reciprocal inclusiveness I am talking about fully symmetrical? Of course, it would not be difficult for us to have a symmetrical situation in the minimal sense that the encounter is equally grudging and limited on both sides.

But the interesting question is whether the encounter is symmetrical in a fuller sense. Is it symmetrical in the sense that each of us believes that my faith includes your faith, yes, but yours includes mine just as fully? And, further, is the situation of encounter symmetrical in the sense that each us says, "My faith rightly judges your faith, but to no greater extent than yours judges mine."

If we have a full symmetry in that sense, then the reciprocal inclusivism we are talking about would not merely be inclusivism. It would be pluralism, because each faith would be equally and independently valid and potent. And that would mean that, on Tillichian grounds, pluralism is true in the very rich sense that we can experience it, certainly at the middle level of our conscious experience, and perhaps at the deep third level as well.

Does this full symmetry obtain? From a "God's-eye perspective" it may be the truth about what is going on in the differing religions. That would mean our differing faiths, when we really understand them and truly believe them, are equally true and equivalently effective. Alternatively, of course, from the God's-eye perspective this perfect symmetry may *not* be the case.

But here is the rub. Even if this symmetry is the case from the transcendent divine point of view, we cannot know it and experience it. We cannot do that because we cannot occupy the divine perspective. We cannot jump out of our finitude. Because we are finite, we have no experiential access, no existential access to the perspective of the transcendent, nor do we have any intercourse with it—except by means of those particular, finite, and concrete symbols in which the infinite makes itself "there" for us. Hence we can never know, experientially and existentially, whether pluralism is true. Or false.

Of course we can guess that it is true. Or false. We can adopt what John Hick very aptly calls "the pluralistic hypothesis."[8] We have seen that Tillich's thought provides for pluralism of this arm's-length, theoretical kind.[9] But Tillich also believes that, when we think, hypothesize, or believe at that objectively detached level—at the level at which we affirm theoretical pluralism—we have abandoned the level of experience at which *religion* "lives and moves and has its being."

If Tillich is right, we cannot say or experience anything that has the transforming breath of the infinite in it except from within the circle of the religion that shapes and determines our reality in depth.[10] We remain limited to the religious symbolism that has thus far "mothered" us—unless and until we are overtaken by some new miracle of revelation, that is, by something like the fresh

---

[8]John Hick, *The Interpretation of Religion*, 233-51.

[9]See pp. 61-64, above.

[10]In this and the next sentence, respectively, I am assuming two Tillichian concepts, that of "the theological circle," ST 1:8-11, and that of "the correlation of revelation," ST 1:126-28.

"breakthrough of the holy ultimate" that I sketched in my imaginary scenario in chapter 4 above.[11]

Thus I conclude that, so long as we hold ourselves to speaking out of a deep level of religious involvement—existentially—we cannot reach pluralism. Maybe God can experience it. But we cannot. Reciprocal inclusivism is as far as we can go.

4. Eschatological Pluralism

We may still want to ask whether there is not some possibility for us to enjoy a pluralist perspective—*other* than in a detached, theoretical, and "onlooker" way.

There is. For most of us I suspect this pluralistic possibility will be a bit equivocal. Still, it may be worth pursuing.

In order to pursue it, we must contrast the equivocal "opening for pluralism" I have in mind with the mystical option that we looked at in the last chapter. There we saw that the mystics are able to drink deeply from the fountain of our Origin. And they are also able to taste hefty drafts of pluralism in the process. But to do that, as we have also seen, they have to turn aside from the rush of history and sink back into the formless, and into formlessness themselves.

Things are otherwise with the pluralist possibility I am now pursuing. This pluralism is something that is the perk of "the activist," as I shall call him.[12] I call him "Activist" because his faith is of a strenuously ethical kind. He is one who rushes into the fray and joins the forward march of history.

But how can this lead to deeply religious experience of a pluralist kind? As we saw in the last chapter, the prophetic-ethical protest is usually *secularizing*.

The full truth is that something different *can* happen. The grand finale of our human venture does not always wait, unseen and unheard, over the horizon. Sometimes the Kingdom of God materializes in our midst, at least in a fragmentary way. Thus, take

---

[11]See pp. 64-65, above.

[12]To preserve gender equality, I use a man as my example here as I used a woman in the preceding chapter as my fictional Buddhist Christian.

courage, Mr. Activist! Because you are on the cutting edge of history, you have a real chance of being at the right place at the right time. The next hurricane that blows in may be a beneficent one. You may be caught up in a genuine kairos.

In such a kairos time, as we have seen, a stupendous number of good things come together. It is even the case that the different types of religion are unified. If our activist has a part in such a moment, the inrushing fullness of the Holy will make all the religions equal right where he lives. Or if these religions are not all exactly equal, it will not make any difference, because they will all be included, topped off for all they are worth. Thus our activist, fully and actively participating in this time, will experience the glad equality of all faiths, and will of course experience their equality at the deepest and most existential level.

But does this hold out much promise? Perhaps it does. Even to those whose faith is not as strenuously active as his, some more modest portion of his rapture may be allotted. Perhaps we all can join in. The reason is that the drive toward ultimacy is real, the infinite is in us, and the ultimate never loses its grip upon us.

And sometimes we feel this. We feel it in a peculiar kind of invitation and promise. It is the promise that somehow, beyond anything we could express or envision, all of those who are grasped by the ultimate mystery, and who truly give themselves to it, will be one—one precisely in their manyness and their diversity.

But this is a fragile vision. Or it is fragile for many people, including myself. I believe it was also fragile for the mature Tillich—though not always for the young Tillich.

So where does this leave us? From time to time this vision may freshen and excite, but I doubt that it is the stuff of which our steady coping and our enduring joy are made.

5. Conclusions for the Chapter and for Part Two

Here I bring part two of this book to a close. I have said a great deal on the subject of "Finding the Best Attitudes in Interreligious Encounters," which of course is the title of part two. In particular, I have employed the thought of Paul Tillich in order to make four proposals that I believe are original.

I bring this chapter to a close by listing and summarizing them. However, the list that follows contains five proposals, not just four. I do not claim the third as original. It is integral to the structure of what I am presenting in this book. Thus I list it and spell it out. But it does not count as one of the "seven original proposals" I mentioned in the preface to this book. I explain why it is not when I reach that proposal.

(1) The familiar three-part typology of interreligious attitudes should be reconstructed in terms of the cognitive levels that Tillich distinguishes. One of the features of this reconstruction is the recognition that the same person can adopt more than one of these attitudes, sometimes almost at the same time.

(2) When the typology is reconstructed in this way, we are able to recognize that there are correlations, or main correlations, between certain cognitive levels and certain interreligious attitudes. These correlations can be detailed in the following way.

Within any interreligious encounter, even if it is only the fleeting encounter of a Christian reading an article on Islam, for example, we may expect the following.

(a) We are likely to experience *pluralist inclinations* at the level at which we engage in detached theoretical or comparative analysis of religions, in empirically objective study of religions, or in relatively casual or social interactions with those from other faiths.

(b) We are likely to sense *inclusivist tendencies* at the middle level at which we share empathetically and perceptively in the different faiths involved in the encounter.

(c) We are likely to feel *exclusivist impulses* and detect *exclusivist implications* at the level at which we sense ourselves existentially involved with our religion. That is the main correlation, I should say. For that relatively small number of people whose piety is predominantly mystical, this level-three correlation is not with exclusivism, but with its opposite, pluralism.

(3) In those situations in which we are engaged in the empirically objective study of religions, or are scrutinizing them in a theoretical and detached manner, or are engaged in casual or social contacts with persons of other faiths, the kind of attitude to be expected and recommended is contextual pluralism.

This proposal is actually a commonplace in the scholarly study of religion, and even in much polite discourse. The only thing original about it is its "contextual" character. But this is the same idea of having an attitude "in certain contexts" that I use in the next proposal. I do not think I can count it twice as something original. Hence I do not count it among my four original proposals in this part of the book.

(4) In certain other kinds of interreligious situations we are well advised to be both ready and able to enter into a contextually exclusivist attitude. The kinds of context in which this is called for are those deeper and more involved encounters in which a concern for being made whole comes to the fore.

Such encounters can arise with considerable frequency in *intra*religious contexts. But in *inter*religious encounters they will be rare. To the extent that they do assert themselves, however, and to the extent that we discern that the symbols, rituals, or transforming message of one given faith are the means by which some kind of existential healing can go forward—and if other involved parties freely invite it—one may engage in existential witness on behalf of that particular religion, and may even sometimes do so in terms of "one way to be saved (in this concrete situation)."

(5) The most central proposal made here with regard to interreligious attitudes is the recommendation that inclusivism, and especially inclusivism of a reciprocal kind, should be one's characteristic or baseline attitude. I think it is the most adequate characteristic or overall attitude. Leaving aside some of the nuances of this attitude for the sake of a compact summary, we can say that it means "I" am convinced that the norm or standard for transforming truth is in "my religion." Otherwise I would not be committed to it as my ultimate concern. Yet I also know—and I *approve* of this fact, at least provisionally!—that "you," if you are a devout and committed adherent of another religion, feel the same about "your faith" in a *reciprocal* way.

My hope in making the proposals in part two of this book is that they will point the way to a more fruitful and a less conflicted way of dealing with the interreligious encounters that have become so important in recent decades. These proposals also summarize and seek to explain a good number of the ideas that Paul Tillich has elaborated in his theological work.

PART THREE

Looking at the Objective, Doctrinal Side

Chapter 8

Is the Christian Message the Only Universal One?

In this chapter and the next—that is, in part three of this book—I turn from the more inward-looking considerations of our attitudes in interreligious encounters to deal with the more outward and objective matters of religious doctrines.

The range of possible topics of this kind is of course vast. The selection I have made will allow us to look, in this chapter, at what might make a religion more apt to be a widespread or even a universal world faith. And in the next chapter, I ask the following question about the nature of ultimate reality as human beings know it and relate to it in the various religions: How personal is ultimate reality?

There is another change of focus at this point in the present book. In the preceding four chapters, I made it a point to deal with Christianity as a religion just as other religions are. No doubt the Christian faith got more attention than the others. But in looking for the best attitudes in interreligious encounters, I was trying to propose things that would apply to any or to all world faiths. I emphasize that I was "trying" to do that. The limits that belong to my social location, personal outlook, and Christian identity have left their mark on the chapters in part two. But the effort was to handle the Christian faith as one faith among others.

In this chapter, by contrast, it is my purpose to focus upon certain things that distinguish Christianity from other faiths, or that distinguish it from some other faiths, in any case. And something else: I offer here a synthesis, an interpretation, and an application of some of the most pro-Christian things Paul Tillich says.

I. The Nature of the Case I Am Making: Why It Is Not Imperialistic

In this chapter I develop the sixth of the seven "original proposals" I mentioned in the preface to this book. It is the proposal that a subtle argument of considerable force is almost explicit in Tillich's thought. This almost-explicit argument is to the effect that the Christian message has a stronger claim to be the universal faith of humankind than does the message of any other faith. For good reasons, an argument of this kind raises the hackles of many generous-spirited and ecumenical people. The apparent imperialism of the argument is offensive, and many of these people are not ready to believe such a spirit is characteristic of Tillich.

They are right about Tillich. Much in this book has already made that fact clear. For that reason, and for other reasons as well, I want to make four points here at the outset, four points I hope will allay if not remove the fears to which I have just referred. In the first three points I shall anticipate some things that will be further explained in this chapter.

(1) If my ecumenical readers are indeed opposed to the domineering self-elevation by which one religion claims to be superior to other religions, then *for that reason* they may like this almost-explicit argument of Tillich's. The reason is that, for Tillich, if a religion is to have the strongest claim to be the universal faith of humankind, it should ideally have the *least* domineering, the *least* arrogant, and the *least* imperialist message of all. It should be the most self-surrendering of all—though that religious message will of course need to have enough historical force to *keep on surrendering itself*, and not just to extinguish itself once and forever.

(2) A religion whose message is most fit to be universal will not give evidence of this fact by subjugating other faiths, much less by obliterating them. The "winner" in this so-called contest among the religions will be the one that can *most fully include*, and *most effectively foster*, all the beneficent and nondestructive manifestations of sacred ultimacy that have appeared in the history of religions. The winner is the most "universal" *in that sense*.

(3) In this argument Tillich draws his conclusions in a pragmatic way from pragmatic criteria. What this means is that his conclusions are not dogmatic declarations. They are invitations. They amount to his saying, "Try it. Run the tests. See if you do not also find these things to be true—though you may have to bet your life for some of it to be true for you."

(4) Finally, and at greatest length, I want to point out that Tillich has made a most important shift in the way he conceives the whole matter of a "contest among the religions." The question with which this chapter is concerned has sometimes been discussed under the heading of "the absoluteness of Christianity."[1] Is Christianity the absolute religion? Are all other faiths merely relative to it? I agree with Tillich that this is a mistaken way to pose the question. The phrase, "the absoluteness of Christianity," is a "not too happy term," Tillich says. He prefers to speak of "the universality of the Christian message, its universal claim."[2]

His point is that Christianity, as a human religion, is not absolute. On the other hand, inasmuch as Christianity's message arises out of an experience of the absolute, all humankind could in principle receive that message and join the chorus—all humankind *universally*.

But can we not say the same thing about other religions, at least as Tillich sees the matter? And if that is the case, is there any good reason to believe that Christianity has a stronger claim to universality than any other faith?

I argue in this chapter that we find in Tillich's thought two criteria for deciding which religion has a message with the stronger claim to be universal, and that when we apply these two criteria in a joint or "interlocking" way—a way I shall explain—the Christian message turns out to have the strongest claim to universality.

2. Two Criteria of Universality

Tillich develops and makes use of at least two principles for judging the potential universality of a religion. I call these principles "criteria of universality." Tillich does not use that term. Neither does he feature them by enshrining them in a list, for

---

[1]Cf. Ernst Troeltsch, *The Absoluteness of Christianity and the History of Religions*, trans. David Reid with an introduction by James Luther Adams (Richmond VA: John Knox Press, 1971); and Ernst Troeltsch, "The Place of Christianity among the World Religions," in *Attitudes toward Other Religions: Some Christian Interpretations*, ed. Owen C. Thomas (New York: Harper & Row, 1969) 73-91.

[2]Paul Tillich, "Missions and World History," in *The Theology of the Christian Mission*, ed. Gerald H. Anderson (New York: McGraw-Hill, 1961) 286.

example. One must dig these criteria out of the way he handles the questions with which the present chapter is concerned.

One of these two criteria is positive, while the other is rather negative. The positive criterion asks whether a religion invests our larger human history with ultimate meaning; and it asks which religion can most adequately do that. I spend most time in this chapter with this positive criterion.

The second or negative criterion asks which religion possesses a superior "guardian"[3] against that religion's own potential for demonic destructiveness. Behind this second criterion lie some of Tillich's ideas that we developed earlier in this book. Every religion has a tendency to claim to be ultimate and absolute in its own right. Secular realities such as nation-states have the same tendency. This tendency is "the demonic,"[4] because when a finite value is made ultimate in this way, it sooner or later becomes destructive of other, competing goods and values in human life.

When I say I apply Tillich's two criteria jointly, or in an "interlocking" way, I mean the following. In agreement with Tillich (ST 3:336-37), I assume that the great world faiths are in a global, history-long "competition" as to which religion is potentially most universal. On the grounds of the first or positive criterion, Christianity proves itself superior to Buddhism. Actually, there is no contest. In Christianity we are given an awareness of the ultimate meaningfulness of our embracing human history, whereas in Buddhism we are not. Buddhism does not even try to do that.

With Buddhism "out of the running," I believe Christianity would be able to "defeat" its remaining rivals on the basis of *either one or both* of the two criteria. However, for the sake of brevity, I deal primarily with the second or negative criterion in the latter part of this chapter. Of course I presuppose what is involved in the

---

[3]I am using this Tillichian term in a partly new way. Tillich develops the idea of "the Guardian" on p. 274 of the response part of his "Religious Symbol," and more extensively in his 1926 "Kairos und Logos," originally translated in Paul Tillich, *The Interpretation of History* (New York: Scribner's, 1936) 171-74. The term is not much used thereafter, apparently because most of what it means is included in Tillich's much-used idea of "the Protestant principle."

[4]Tillich, "On the Boundary: An Autobiographical Sketch," in his *The Interpretation of History*, 25-26; cf. ST 1:217-18.

positive criterion. Thus, in the latter parts of the chapter, in sections 5 and 6, I try to show that (according to Tillich) the Christian message has the power to invest human history with ultimate meaning while, at the same time, it possesses a guardian (the crucified Christ) that protects people from the demonic destructiveness sometimes fomented by Christianity itself. Moreover, this guardian is superior to what we find in other religions, Buddhism excepted.

Beyond the two criteria I have identified, one may find Tillich using others. The two I have chosen are sufficient for my purposes, however. They also appear to be the least questionable and the strongest, especially if one applies them in the interlocking way I have just explained.[5]

3. The Relation between Center and Meaning

To begin our consideration of the positive criterion, we ask how "the meaning of history" arises. Tillich believes that human beings' awareness that their history is meaningful enters decisively into their affairs in an event that is, for the larger community to which they belong, the "center" of their history. When he speaks in this way of history, he has in mind a two-phase structure or gestalt.[6] At the center of this gestalt is a turning point from the predominantly "questioning" first phase of history to the second phase. In the second phase, our life together is still beset by questions, but the way we experience our corporate existence is also qualified by a sense that an "answer" to our questionings has been received, or has at least been identified. It is the center of history that brings this answer.

---

[5]Tillich believes a universal faith must manifest a salvation that is of grace, and not merely a salvation that comes through doing the works prescribed by some religious law. He finds Islam lacking on this score. He apparently also finds Judaism lacking in this respect as well. See ST 3:368-69. I think it would be hard to defend some of Tillich's claims at this point. In the same place, but making a different point, he also says Judaism cannot be a universal faith because "its universality has not yet been liberated from its particularity" (ST 3:368).

[6]"[H]uman history, seen from the point of view of the self-transcendence of history, is not only a dynamic movement, running ahead, but also a structured whole in which one point is the center" (ST 3:366).

Among other things, this center brings into focus a goal or telos for the larger human enterprise, and injects into human experience the energizing conviction that this telos will somehow be reached. As is apparent, the gestalt I have just described is the two-ages eschatological faith of the New Testament in outline.[7]

In this way we can understand what it means to speak of "the meaning of history." The centered, two-phase gestalt defines a "macroplot" according to which the course of human events makes narrative sense. Large questions begin to stir at the dim origins of this process. These questions or "questings" initiate a preparatory period in which sensitive souls are groping for answers. There then appears a plot-defining center or turning point. And that center sets in motion a march toward the now-anticipated denouement.[8]

But is this macroplot a plot for the total human story, or is it a plot only for some less-inclusive group during some less-than-total stretch or strand of events? The answer to that question is twofold. (a) In the first place, such a plot can be either partial or total. Virtually everyone lives in more than one meganarrative at a time, and some of those narratives are more inclusive than others. But the second answer to the question just asked is more interesting. (b) Some partial plots expand into total plots.

We may explain this by pointing first to the way Tillich speaks of the "vocational consciousness" one finds in empires or nations.[9] When a powerful nation-state or a successful empire comes up with a sense of its own vocation or mission, it is almost inevitable that this historical group will see its role on the stage of history as

---

[7]Perhaps it is clearest in Paul. See 1 Corinthians 10:11 and 15:20-28, for example.

[8]My use of narrative categories here points to the fact that Tillich is a narrative theologian of consequence. Narrative theology is a many-splendored thing, of course; and what Tillich offers is but one kind. But it is a subtle and compelling kind. See Gary L. Comstock, "Two Types of Narrative Theology," *Journal of the American Academy of Religion* 55 (Winter 1987): 687-717, and in *Why Narrative?* ed. Stanley Hauerwas and L. Gregory Jones (Grand Rapids MI: Eerdmans, 1989) 1-18.

[9]Tillich discusses eight Western examples of a "vocational consciousness," from Alexander the Great to the United States, in his *Love, Power, and Justice* (New York: Oxford University Press, 1954) 101-104, and approximately the same ones again at ST 3:340, 349.

the starring role. For that reason, the group will typically view its own story as the center of the entire historical process. Its mission is the clue that gives meaning to the total human venture. Prior to the emergence of this historical group, humanity was in a time of waiting, though people generally would have had little awareness of what they were waiting for. But now that the favored empire has appeared—or now that some other vanguard of the future has appeared—history has received its plot, the meaning and goal of human existence comes into focus, and the Grand March toward the final destiny of humankind is under way.

4. The Meaningfulness of History as a Criterion: Buddhism

Although the kinds of macroplots and meganarratives I am talking about have enormous creative power, they also have great destructive or demonic potential as well. One thinks of the shadow side of European colonialism, and of the shadow side of the American sense of "manifest destiny." And one thinks of the sense of national mission epitomized in the Nazi idea of "The Third Reich."

All this raises a question. Would not our race be better off if we were able to stifle all the grandiose ideas of the meaning of history, and throttle every impulse to believe that the center of history has appeared?

It could never be done. The conviction that history is meaningful is not something it would be nice merely for some elite group to enjoy. If *people generally* do not sense some such direction in their collective lives, they cannot feel and decide from day to day that the larger dimensions of the events in which their lives are caught up *make sense*. And without the kind of center that makes such a plot convincing, the larger, enveloping occurrences in human life will be felt, at best, to be "going nowhere." At worst, they will be experienced as a menacing chaos or an ironically if not a maliciously concatenated sequence of happenings.

The previous paragraph is one rendering of Tillich's doctrine that we humans are historical beings in the very strong sense that we have our *full being as human* only as participants in the experience of history-bearing groups. History is not just an essential dimension of our being. History is also the most inclusive dimension.[10] Human beings do not live by bread alone. They also thirst for meaning in their history. And they will find it, willy-nilly, for better or for worse.

Thus, to whatever extent any religion speaks of a salvation that does *not* importantly involve answers concerning the ultimate pointlessness or the ultimate sense of the political, societal, inter-national, and global features of our life together, to that extent that particular religion fails to speak of a salvation for the entirety of what makes us human. A religion that is nonhistorical in this sense can speak of fulfillment only for some more-or-less abstractly isolated *aspects or ingredients* of the human reality.

In Tillich's view, Buddhism is the clearest example, among the great world faiths, of a faith that is not universal on these grounds. No doubt Tillich fails to give all strands of that tradition their due; but, as he plausibly understands the matter, the tradition of Sakyamuni cannot offer full salvation or fulfillment for our total human reality, including our historical reality, because Buddhism does not even try to do that: the ultimate fulfillment it seeks, embodies, and offers is a fulfillment "above" or "from out of" the concrete history in which we humans are embroiled. Neither Buddhist Enlightenment nor Nirvana is vested in historical occurrences. That is, Buddhism does not expect anything ulti-mately meaningful to take hold of human life and fulfill itself in and through the purposive, ongoing, corporately social novelties *and attachments* that constitute the humanly historical process (ST 3:368-69; cf. ST 1:120-21).

This first criterion also includes the proposition that a historical faith in the sense I have explained can incorporate nonhistorical salvation, but not the reverse. Tillich is quite clear in maintaining this proposition. He understands it as a basis for Christianity's claim to be a, if not the, universal type of religion (ST 2:89). To speak in Christian terms: in the fragmentary historical appearances of the Kingdom of God in history there is ample room for subjects of that Kingdom to experience Eternal Life in nonhistorical as well

---

[10]Paul Tillich, "Dimensions, Levels, and the Unity of Life," *Kenyon Alumni Bulletin* (Kenyon College, Gambier OH) 17 (October–December 1958): 4-8; ST 3:25-26, 297-99. See also Tillich, "Religion und Weltpolitik," GW 9:176-77.

as in historical terms; but a nonhistorical Eternal Life could not embody the historical, narrative meaningfulness that is conveyed by the idea of the Kingdom of God.

5. The Center of History in Jesus Received as the Christ

Our discussion of the center and meaning of history has thus far dealt with those realities largely in general terms. I want now to deal with the center and meaning of history as Christians experience these things—as Christians experience them and invite others also to experience them. My purpose, as I say earlier in this chapter, is to make clear the power of the Christian message to fill human history with meaning as Tillich views the matter.

For Tillich, as for the New Testament, the concrete center of the whole of human history is the event of Jesus received as the Christ, that is, Jesus received as the bringer of the new aeon of salvation. This new aeon is the second phase of the gestalt we discussed earlier. To live in it is to be graciously grasped by the event that sets this stage of history in motion. It is to experience a healing in principle—that is, a healing in beginning and in power—of all the existential ugliness we humans suffer: the estrangement, the ambiguity, the threats to our wholeness, the self-destructiveness, and the pointlessness or hopelessness of having no fulfilling historical telos in front of us. It is to participate in New Being in contrast with the old being of the first phase of history (ST 1:126-28, 137-39; 3:362-67).[11]

I have just spoken of salvation. I could have spoken of revelation, because the two are coterminous for Tillich. Where we have one we have the other. Revelation is not sacred information that might or might not be useful someday if we decided to "get saved." Rather, revelation is the impact in our awareness of our actually participating in salvation. It is the cognitive side of our

---

[11]In order to put Tillich's precise idea across in English, I speak here of "New Being" rather than of "*the* New Being." It is quite true that Tillich used the latter expression when he spoke and wrote in English. The expression is a Germanicism, however, and it tends either to baffle the native English speaker or to convey an idea Tillich did not intend.

participating in New Being. Thus the two-phase history of salvation is at the same time the two-phase history of revelation (ST 1:144-47).

Tillich calls the center of this structure "final revelation." Revelation given in Jesus received as the Christ is final and unsurpassable for anyone who is grasped and transformed through the Christian symbols, notably, through the Crucifixion and Resurrection of Christ. Even the goal of history is the fulfillment of what became manifest and effective at the center of history in Jesus accepted as the Christ. For that reason it can be called "final revelation" (ST 1:137).

Because Tillich speaks of unsurpassable revelation in Christ in this way, he is sometimes thought to be simply and unqualifiedly an exclusivist.[12] But Tillich believes revelation and salvation are present beyond the circle of the Christian community. This we have already seen in chapters two and three above; but the notion is important here, too. We cannot understand his notion of the center of history without it.

Speaking of the revelation and salvation that are present in non-Christian communities, Tillich says these people participate to some extent in the unambiguous life of the "Spiritual Community." However, non-Christians belong only to the latent and not to the manifest Spiritual Community. That is, from a Christian perspective, they inhabit phase one of the gestalt I discuss in section 3 of this chapter. Communities of non-Christian people receive revelation, true, but it is preparatory and anticipatory. By contrast, the community that lives in history's second phase is in process of receiving revelation that is dependent upon, and not simply preparatory for, final revelation (ST 1:136-37, 2:118-20, 135-36, 3:149-55).

The contrast between phase-one communities and the phase-two community is not absolute. From a certain point of view, however, it is decisive. I need to say a word about both the non-absoluteness and the decisiveness of this contrast.

This contrast is not absolute because, even in the manifest Spiritual Community that Christian churches are supposed to constitute, there are enormous distortions. There is pervasive am-

---

[12]See p. 54, above.

biguity. These evils partly relativize the contrast between phase-one communities and the phase-two community.

On the other hand, the contrast involved here is decisive—from the point of view of one who is aware of belonging to the second phase of the gestalt called "history." This fact is neither strange nor incoherent. To dwell within the second phase of history is to be aware that one is a recipient of final revelation. If we found this revelation to be surpassable, then obviously it would not be for us divine revelation. And it would certainly not be final revelation: it would not be an awareness of being ultimately, unconditionally, totally, and infinitely concerned. Rather, it would be something like a goad that could do no more than prompt us to look for something more—for something that, in principle, would be better.

Nevertheless, there is an important footnote to be added to the decisiveness of this contrast between people in phase one and people in phase two. Just as I may view a Muslim, for example, as in the preparatory phase of history that is destined to find its authentic fulfillment in the Christian revelation, so the Muslim will return the compliment: he or she will see me in the preparatory first phase of history that will come to fulfillment only in Islam. And I take Islam as an illustration here of other ways of affirming the ultimate meaningfulness of human history.

I have already dealt with this kind of situation. I did so in my discussion of "reciprocal inclusivism" in chapter 7. However, I dealt only with some aspects of the all-important historical dimension there.[13]

6. Which Guardian Proves Best? The Second Criterion

Earlier, in section 4 of this chapter, I took note of the demonic destruction that ensues when one historical community's meganarrative is taken to be the ultimate and unconditional meaning of all human history. Of course, demonic destructiveness makes itself felt not just in the historical sphere, but also in every aspect of life, for example, in the individual's psyche, and in the smaller groupings

---

[13]See pp. 116-19 in the preceding chapter.

to which the individual belongs. But clearly there is something especially dangerous about the meganarratives and macroplots that unify the energies and resources of millions of people.

Accordingly, the second of the criteria of which I have spoken is that a universal faith must have an inbuilt guardian, something that will, at least in principle, protect that religion against the demonic tendency that lurks in all religion. So far as this second criterion is concerned, the more effective a religion's guardian is, the more compelling is its claim to be universal.

This is a point at which one could say that Buddhism is superior to Christianity. The paradigmatic story of the Buddha, his teachings, and the spiritual disciplines of the Eightfold Path are a powerful guardian against the lofty pretensions of any person, group, or cause, certainly including any cause that is enshrined in a historical group's meganarrative. Judged by this criterion alone, in fact, and judged by the history of the peoples and cultures that have been strongly shaped respectively by Buddhism or by Christianity, I would say that Buddhism has the superior claim to being the most universal religion.

But this is also the point at which I make an interlocking application of my two criteria. Having used the first criterion to eliminate Buddhism from the "competition to be the most universal faith," I am now prepared to use the second, negative criterion (on which Buddhism might be superior) to eliminate the rest.

I think one could also make the same case on the basis of the first or positive criterion. That is, one could plausibly argue that Christianity excels all religions, and not just Buddhism, in its capacity to infuse narrative meaning into history. But I take the shortest route to the goal I wish to reach. I deal directly only with the second criterion, the positive criterion that speaks of the meaning of history.

But is there any way to rank the world religions with regard to this second criterion—or the first, for that matter? According to Tillich, there is. Where he is discussing the question of verifying basic philosophical principles, he considers the pragmatic test: Which principles work? Which ones succeed? He rejects the pragmatism of a narrow instrumental test, but he goes on to recognize that philosophical systems have throughout history been accepted and rejected according to a process that employs both rational and pragmatic elements. It is an inexact and indefinite process, he acknowledges, but it nevertheless "throws out of the historical process what is exhausted and powerless and what cannot stand in the light of pure rationality" (ST 1:105).

Tillich clearly gives great weight here to what we might call the historical-pragmatic test, a test in which principles can be verified according to their "efficacy in the life-process of mankind" (ST 1:105, cf. 1:104). In a kind of thought experiment, I want to apply this historical-pragmatic test to the Christian understanding of the center of history.

Invoking the plot line of the Gospel of Mark (which constitutes much of the plot line of the other gospels as well, of course), Tillich argues that Jesus—the Jesus we meet as the Christ in the biblical picture of him—would not let himself be recognized as the history-ruling Christ except through the complete surrender of himself as a finite human individual (Mark 8:27-33).

In this same Markan context, Jesus proceeds to tell Peter that he is demonic ("Get behind me, Satan!") when Peter tries to persuade Jesus to avoid the cross.[14] From this and other biblical themes, Tillich develops his well-known contention that the biblical Jesus was the Christ in three respects, namely, (1) by virtue of "the undisrupted unity of the center of his being with God," (2) by virtue of the way he "preserves this unity against all the attacks coming from estranged existence," and (3) by virtue of "the self-surrendering love" (ST 2:138) in which he made a "continuous sacrifice of himself as Jesus to himself as the Christ" (ST 1:137, cf. 135-37), that is, by virtue of "the continuous sacrifice of himself as a particular individual under the conditions of existence to himself as the bearer of the New Being" (ST 2:123).

In this understanding of the center of history, Christianity has an immensely powerful guardian against the demonic. Admittedly, Christianity has wrought a huge share of the havoc brought upon the world through its arrogance and its religious triumphalism. But in principle, and with Buddhism out of the picture, it is difficult to

---

[14]Paul Tillich, *The Shaking of the Foundations* (New York: Scribner's, 1948) 146-47; idem, *The Theology of Culture* (New York: Oxford University Press, 1959) 67.

imagine how one could find another central religious symbol in a great world faith that can match the potential of "Jesus the crucified received as the Christ," thus understood. And it is by no means merely Tillich who understands this Jesus so. Witness the New Testament.

There are several places where Tillich says Christianity must negate itself as a religion.[15] This is sometimes taken to mean Tillich is flatly pluralistic. Granted, there is a pluralistic element at work. I have tried to deal with it earlier in this book, especially in chapter 4. But when Tillich speaks in this way, his deeper point is sometimes—and the deeper implication of what he is saying is always—that Christianity is the strongest contender for the status of a universal faith because, precisely in being itself, that is, precisely in proclaiming its own unique message, it proves itself most able to negate itself as a finite religion in favor of the absolute transcendent. The historical-pragmatic test thus amounts to the following. Let us try, and let us see. Can any other faith, Buddhism excepted, match what Christianity is able to do in this regard?

---

[15]Tillich, *Christianity and the Encounter of World Religions* (1963) 96-97; (1994) 61-62; Tillich, *The Encounter of Religions and Quasi-Religions*, 73-74.

Chapter 9

Is Ultimate Reality Personal?
Adding Buber to Tillich

One of the main issues dividing one religious tradition from another is the question whether ultimate reality is personal or impersonal. John Hick devotes two chapters of his *An Interpretation of Religion*, respectively, to precisely this difference, one chapter to religious traditions in which ultimate reality is encountered and understood as personal, and the next chapter to religions in which ultimate reality is known as impersonal.[1] And the distinction is a commonplace in the study of the religions of the world.[2]

On which side of this divide does Paul Tillich fall? Is Tillich's God personal or impersonal? As we shall see, it is not possible to give a clear-cut, either/or answer to that question. From my point of view, however, Tillich's deity is *not sufficiently* personal. I have a very serious difference with him at this very basic point.

For that reason, I do something in this chapter that is different from what I have done in the previous chapters. Until now, with the exception of some footnotes, I have recommended almost everything in Tillich's thought with which I have dealt. In some cases I have even gone further than that. When I have not found Tillich saying something directly on this or that issue—especially on the "exclusivism-inclusivism-pluralism" typology—I have sought to work out and recommend the implications of some of Tillich's basic concepts and insights. In short, I have written thus far mostly as a Tillichian.

In this chapter, by contrast, I offer a "revisionist Tillichian" perspective. As the last of my seven original proposals in this book,

---

[1]See John Hick, *An Interpretation of Religion* (New Haven CT and London: Yale University Press, 1989) 245-49, and then chap. 15, "The *Personae* of the Real," 252-77, and chap. 16, "The *Impersonae* of the Real," 278-96.

[2]Owen Thomas calls attention to the distinction in Max Weber and Peter Berger in Owen C. Thomas, "Christianity and the Perennial Philosophy," *Theology Today* 43/2 (1986): 259-66.

I propose a very basic change in Tillich's theory of reality. Let me explain a bit further what I am changing, the way I am changing it, and why I am doing so.

The thing I am changing is Tillich's "model of the real," that is, the basic representation of reality as an operating system that we find in Tillich's ontological concepts and key ontological metaphors.[3] Though I recoil from Tillich at one very basic point—originally I felt threatened by him at this point—I am fascinated and considerably influenced by his daring metaphysical vision. I believe the concepts and metaphors in which he has spelled out this "model of reality" are illuminating and useful, up to the point noted.

The way I change this ontological model is to take something new and different and insert it into what Tillich calls "the basic ontological structure." This new and different thing is a certain understanding of our I-Thou encounter with God and with our fellow human beings. I understand this I-Thou relation, and the contrasting "I-It world," substantially in the sense of Martin Buber[4] and his "dialogical philosophy."[5]

---

[3]Two key loci are ST 1:163-204 and 3:11-32.

[4]As the basic text, I have employed Martin Buber, *Ich und Du*, in Buber's *Die Schriften über das Dialogische Prinzip* (Heidelberg: Verlag Lambert Schneider, 1954) 5-121. Generally I quote from Buber's *I and Thou*, 2nd [British] ed. with a postscript by the author, trans. Ronald Gregor Smith (Edinburgh: T. & T. Clark, 1959; ©1958); henceforth cited as Buber, *I and Thou*. I have also made use of Walter Kaufmann's translation and notes: Martin Buber, *I and Thou. A New Translation with a Prologue "I and You" and Notes*, by Walter Kaufmann (New York: Charles Scribner's Sons, 1970).

In addition to citing page numbers, I identify sections of the book, e.g., "Buber, *I and Thou*, 4, §2." One may note the sections of *I and Thou* are not numbered; they are, however, marked and separated by certain printer's symbols (variously, stars [or asterisks], diamonds, or bullets). Smith's original translation puts §§4 and 5 together as a single section. My numbering splits that "section" and counts its pieces 4 and 5.

[5]Michael Theunissen, "The Philosophy of Dialogue as the Counterproject to Transcendental Philosophy: The Dialogic of Martin Buber," pt. 3 of Michael Theunissen, *The Other: Studies in the Social Ontology of Husserl, Heidegger, Sartre, and Buber*, trans. Christopher Macann with an introduction by Fred R. Dallmayr (Cambridge MA: MIT Press, 1984) 257-384.

The reason I make this change, as I have indicated, is in order that God may be understood as fully personal—that is, in order that God may be the Eternal Thou by whom we human beings are encountered and addressed at the most ultimate level, I to Thou.[6]

I. Tillich's God: Personal Enough?

It has to be acknowledged, however, that Tillich's God is in a very significant sense already personal. As he says, "God is the ground of everything personal and . . . carries within himself the ontological power of personality. He is not a person, but he is not less than personal" (ST 1:245). Thus the focal question at issue could be phrased, "To what degree and in what senses should God be recognized as personal?" That still is a question of immense importance, however, as I hope to show.

I should also say I have no special quarrel with those who find the Tillichian deity personal enough. I would be pleased to persuade them differently, but I do not deny that their position is, for example, a Christian option; and I certainly have no complaint when they use Tillich's compelling model of reality to work out their kind of faith in God. The model was made more for them than for me.

My problem—and here my mediating approach comes to the fore—is that I want to make use of Tillich's conceptuality, too; and if his model must be revised to make that possible I say, So be it!

---

[6]One of the more recent to criticize Tillich for the nonpersonalness of his God is Oswald Bayer. I have serious problems with Bayer's account of Tillich's thought, but I do not think he greatly overstates one aspect of the matter when he says that "Tillich's theology is in a decisive respect a polemic against the philosophical and theological personalism of this century, against talk of 'I and Thou' and of the 'encounter' between God and humanity." Bayer, *Theologie*, vol. 1 of *Handbuch systematischer Theologie*, ed. Carl Heinz Ratschow (Gütersloh: Gütersloher Verlagshaus, 1994) 241 (my trans.), cf. 185-280. See also Guy B. Hammond, "Tillich on the Personal God," *Journal of Religion* 46 (October 1964): 289-93. Though the essentials of my analysis in this chapter were worked out independently of Hammond—they were submitted in my doctoral dissertation before Hammond's article appeared—my analysis is similar to his. Hammond takes no stand for or against Tillich's view in his article, however. In particular, he proposes no revisions.

I also do not believe my revision diminishes the profundity, verve, or coherence of Tillich's metaphysical vision. What it does do, besides "thickening" the model in which his vision is epitomized, is to expand that model's scope—to expand it in such a way that the model can interpret (without prejudice!) a wider range of religious experience, notably including the experience of those who sense themselves confronted and addressed, at the most ultimate level, I-to-thou, by the living, speaking God of the biblical witness.

2. I-Thou in Tillich and Buber

There is a notion of I-Thou encounter in Tillich, and it plays a significant role in his systematic theology. Though it differs from Buber's ideas, as we shall see, Tillich gives Buber credit for precipitating this "I-Thou" in his own systematic thinking. It happened, Tillich tells us, during "two evenings of dialogue" with Buber in New York when the two men were refugees from Nazi Germany. "[W]hat I learned [from this dialogue], and used later in my ethical writings," Tillich says, "is the insight that the moral imperative and its unconditioned character are identical with the demand that I acknowledge every person as person, every 'thou' as a 'thou,' and that I am acknowledged in the same way."[7]

In Tillich's own developed I-Thou doctrine, the person "is established in the encounter of an ego-self with another self, often called the 'I-thou' relationship, and it [the person] exists only in community with other persons."[8] As Tillich explains this: though we human beings transcend ourselves indefinitely in all directions as we know and control ourselves and the contents of our world, and though we are limited in this venture only by our finitude, "there is one limit to man's attempt to draw all content into himself—the other self." We can destroy it as a self if we are

---

[7]Paul Tillich, "Martin Buber," in *The Essential Tillich*, ed. F. Forrester Church (New York: Collier-Macmillan, 1987) 230. According to GW 14:236 this memorial address was first published in *Martin Buber, 1878–1965, An Appreciation of His Life and Thought* (New York: American Friends of the Hebrew University, 1965) 10-13.

[8]Paul Tillich, *Biblical Religion and Ultimate Reality* (Chicago: University of Chicago Press, 1955) 23.

powerful enough, but we cannot assimilate it as a content of our world: we cannot assimilate it in its status as a free, intelligent, and centered self. We can only acknowledge it (ST 3:40).

Further, in two brief assessments of Buber's I-and-Thou ideas, one in 1948 and the other in 1952, Tillich speaks entirely in positive terms.[9] Especially in the 1948 assessment he reproduces several of Buber's ideas about the contrast between I-Thou and I-It, and explains how they are significant for theological work. The pithiest phrase comes in 1952 when Tillich says Buber's "doctrine of the I-Thou correlation between God and man . . . has become a common good of Protestant Theology and it is still increasing in significance."[10]

3. Critique of Tillich's Criticisms of Buber

Despite this appreciation for Buber, Tillich does not align himself with some of Buber's chief ideas, notably, not with the idea that I-Thou encounters are direct and unmediated.[11] And, more to the point, there are two places in the literature where Tillich expresses serious misgivings about Buber's view.

One of these places is a paper Tillich published in 1956. There he refers to Buber's "famous phrase, 'the I-Thou relationship,' " and says it "*can* be understood in essentialist terms and can be used as a descriptive feature, showing how the ego becomes an ego only in the encounter with another ego in which it finds its limit and is thrown back upon itself." As we have seen, Tillich understands and employs Buber's famous phrase in this way.

"Yet," Tillich continues, "it was an existentialist invasion when Buber tried to remove the universals from the encounter between

---

[9]Paul Tillich, "An Evaluation of Martin Buber: Protestant and Jewish Thought," in Tillich, *Theology of Culture*, ed. Robert C. Kimball (New York: Oxford University Press, 1959) 189-92; this article was first published in *Commentary* 5 (June 1948). See also Tillich, "Jewish Influences on Contemporary Christian Theology," *Cross Currents* 2 (Spring 1952): 38-40.

[10]Tillich, "Jewish Influences," 38.

[11]Buber, *I and Thou*, 11-12, 15.

ego and thou, and to make both speechless, for there are no words for the absolute particular, the other ego."[12]

Tillich is not doing justice to Buber here. According to Buber, it is *precisely in our "speaking"*—that is, in one of the two primary words (*Grundworte*), "I-Thou"—that we relate to a Thou. And Buber leaves no doubt that this is something that belongs to our essential nature as human beings.[13] Further, one burden of Buber's little *I and Thou* is to show that primary words, especially "I-Thou," are ontologically prior to and give rise to human egos,[14] just as these primary words also give rise to the language these egos speak, including the language in which universals figure.[15] In Tillich's terminology, Buber's primary I-Thou word is an a priori ontological structure. Buber himself calls it "the *a priori* of relation, *the inborn Thou*."[16] (I return to this point in section 6 below.)

Tillich's "existentialist invasion" criticism of Buber invites one further comment. When Tillich says the ego is speechless before the absolute particular, the other ego, Tillich displays some inattentiveness (if not a degree of deafness) to a difference that is absolutely basic in Buber, namely, the difference between second-person and third-person speech. Even if it were true that Buber's doctrine strips from every Thou the qualities we could conceptualize in universals—and I do not believe it is true—that would only suspend our capacity to talk *about* the other in third-person speech. It would not touch our capacity, or our calling, to speak *to* the

---

[12]Paul Tillich, "Existential Analyses and Religious Symbols," in *Four Existentialist Theologians*, ed. Will Herberg (Garden City NY: Doubleday, 1958) 279-80. According to Herberg's note (277n.), this article was first published in *Contemporary Problems in Religion*, ed. Harold A. Basilius (Detroit: Wayne University Press, 1956) 37-55.

[13]"[W]ithout *It* man cannot live. But he who lives with *It* alone is not a man." Buber, *I and Thou*, 34, cf. 30.

[14]Buber, *Ich und Du* 7, 2, "Grundworte sagen nicht etwas aus, was außer ihnen bestünde, sondern gesprochen stiften sie einen Bestand." Translator Smith, I think, largely misses the point: "Primary words do not describe something that might exist independently of them, but being spoken they bring about existence" (p. 3). Kaufmann translates: "Primary words do not state something that might exist outside them; by being spoken they establish a mode of existence" (p. 53).

[15]Buber, *I and Thou* 24-33, sects. 27-29.

[16]Buber, *I and Thou*, 27, sect. 27.

other, to address the other, and to relate to the other. That is something we do in second-person speech, "you," and we may do it even if the one who stands there is absolutely particular—as indeed he or she is.

The second place in the literature where Tillich expresses serious reservations about Buber's I-Thou ideas is in the same 1965 memorial address in which he says the two-evening dialogue with Buber in New York prompted his I-Thou ideas. To understand the misgivings about Buber that Tillich expresses in this place, we need to know that Tillich is still reacting, in 1965, to something Buber said back in 1924. In 1924 Tillich had delivered a paper proposing that, for the Religious Socialist movement, traditional religious terms should be replaced, including the word "God." "After I finished," says Tillich, "Martin Buber arose and attacked what he called the 'abstract facade' I had built. With great passion, he said that there are some aboriginal words like 'God,' which cannot be replaced at all."[17]

Tillich accepted Buber's point about "God," but he never accepted what Buber said about a facade. Tillich speaks as follows in the 1965 address about his two-evening New York dialogue with Buber back in the Nazi era.

> This dialogue was one of the most important I ever had. It dealt with the question of how far Buber's I-Thou encounter, contrasted to the I-It relation, is an exact description of what really happens in the encounter of person with person. I asked (in a hidden defense of my conceptual facade many years ago) whether one can say that there is a *"pure I"* that relates to a *"pure Thou."* Or whether there is a particular "Thou" with qualities, different or opposed, but equally able to be conceptualized; for instance as a male, a European, a Jew of the twentieth century, an intellectual, et cetera.[18]

In these words Tillich rejects Buber's unmediated I-Thou encounter because it would be a meeting between "pure egos," that is, egos stripped of the qualities that give them their identities as

---

[17]Tillich, "Martin Buber," 229.
[18]Tillich, "Martin Buber," 229-30.

particular beings. Further, since Tillich believes these qualities can be conceptualized, and since he does not believe the concepts in which that happens are a mere facade—they "describe the structure of the building itself," as he puts it[19]—it follows that these conceptualized qualities are objective. They are our objectification of our Thou. And that means the other human person is our object even during the course of our I-Thou encounter with him or her.

4. Is Tillich's I-Thou Authentic?

From Buber's perspective, and even from Tillich's, this last conclusion raises a suspicion. Buber insists that any being we are objectifying is an It, not a Thou, and that it is a melancholy fate that our Thou's must all become It's or objects.[20] Tillich agrees, at least when he is looking at things in a more sociological and a less individual perspective. It is utterly characteristic of Tillich when he deplores what he calls "the tendency of the industrial society . . . to transform everything into an object, an 'It', as Buber says."[21] Given these perspectives of both Buber and Tillich, the suspicion that arises is as follows. Because Tillich believes that our Thou is our object even while we are in I-Thou relation to it, is there something inauthentic about his I-Thou doctrine?

Tillich is able to allay this suspicion, but (if I may put it this way) he has to call upon nothing less than God to remedy the situation. "[T]here is no other way of becoming an 'I,' " he writes, "than by meeting a 'Thou' and by accepting it as such, and there is no other way of meeting and accepting a 'Thou' than by meeting and accepting the 'eternal Thou' in the finite 'Thou.' "[22]

Here Tillich tells us that, when we meet a Thou and acknowledge it as such, we run headlong into (so I read him) the seething, empowering, commanding, sacred depth of life. That is, we run into God *in* the other; and that is what makes a given encounter an I-Thou relation rather than *simply* one more of our objectifications of the contents of our world. The underlying fact is that God

---

[19]Tillich, "Martin Buber," 230.
[20]Buber, *I and Thou*, 12-13, 17; 16-18, 22.
[21]Tillich, "Jewish Influences," 38.
[22]Tillich, "An Evaluation of Martin Buber," 189.

cannot be objectified; God is beyond the subject-object structure; and thus when we meet and accept the Eternal Thou in the finite other we mutually participate in that finite other at a level that transcends the subject-object structure. In that way, and only in that way, our relationship with that finite Thou partakes of unconditionality, or is suffused with the breath of God and lifted to I-Thou status.

Although what I have just described is an estimable I-Thou doctrine, it is easy to feel that something is missing. Whereas in Tillich the I-Thou does not happen until we are drawn and driven past our particular objectified Thou into the depths we share with that Thou, in Buber it is precisely the concrete individuality of our Thou—its absolute particularity—that beckons us to God and opens God to us. As Buber puts it, "The extended lines of relations meet in the eternal *Thou*. Every particular *Thou* [!] is a glimpse through to the eternal *Thou*; by means of every particular *Thou* the primary word addresses the eternal *Thou*."[23]

5. Why Real (Buberian) I-Thou Cannot Happen in Tillich

In this chapter I have said a good many things about how knowledge works in the Tillichian universe. For example, I have described the way—for Tillich but not for Buber—we objectify the Thou's we encounter in our world. But in order to move further, I want to refer again to the short article that was so important for my discussion back in chapter 4, especially in sections 3 and 4. That article is entitled "Participation and Knowledge: Problems of an Ontology of Cognition."[24]

As we saw in chapter 4, we as knowing subjects never know anything without the involvement of two opposite elements, separation and participation. Our separation is our objectifying some-

---

[23]Buber, *I and Thou*, 75, 44.

[24]Paul Tillich, "Participation and Knowledge: Problems of an Ontology of Cognition (1955)," MW 1:381-89. I believe English-language Tillich scholarship was handicapped for decades by the fact that this lucid little essay was until 1989 available in English only in a remote German serial, *Sociologica*.

thing, our keeping our subjectivity out of it, our holding it at a distance, or our just being remote from whatever it is we know about.

Our participation, on the other hand, can mean that to a considerable degree we are merged into something, or that our very life is tied up with it. That would be existential or religious awareness; it would be encounter in depth. Or, secondly, our participation can amount to something very thin and "surface," as in the detached knowledge of the sciences. Or, in the third place, there may be something like a balance of separation and participation. These balanced or in-between sorts of knowing might be our understanding a friend, our understanding a language, our interpreting a novel, or our coming to insight into our own psyche.

Thus we observed the three Tillichian depths or levels of encounter. The rule is that the more deeply we know something, the larger the degree of participation we have in it, whereas the more superficial or theoretical our knowledge of something, the more separation and objectification are at work. But there is always some of each.

In knowing, we oscillate back and forth between two opposite kinds of moments, namely, moments in which "uniting participation" predominates, and moments in which "separating objectivation" predominates (MW 1:389). The depth at which our knowledge of an other takes place depends upon the relative predominance of one or the other of these moments in the unfolding oscillation: are the recurring *uniting-participating* moments longer, stronger, and more intense; or are the *separating-objectivating* moments longer, stronger, and more intense; or are the two more or less equally pronounced?

The reason for reviewing this Tillich doctrine is that it is an obvious verbalization of a mental model; and that model, as I hope now to show, makes it clear that there is no ontological place—no possibility—for the direct, nonobjectifying I-to-Thou relation about which Buber speaks so movingly.

We may visualize the experience of knowing, as Tillich analyzes it, as an undulating line that moves through time in a succession of waves. The trough of each wave represents the moment of maximum participation involved in some instance of knowing, while the peak of each wave represents the moment of maximum separation and objectivation. To be sure, I could have used "peak" and "trough," or "up" and "down," with an opposite orientation; but the orientation I have adopted fits Tillich's language better.

It is important that this graph, together with the model it expresses, has only two axes. Along the Time axis, an experience of knowing moves "forward" from moment to moment; and as it does so, it undulates "up and down" along the other axis, from the high of maximum separation to the low of maximum participation and back again.

How does this show that real I-Thou encounter, by which I mean Buberian I-Thou encounter, is ruled out? When we place a finger on a "lowest point" on this curve—that is, on a moment of maximum participation—we touch a part of the curve at which, for at least a faint and fleeting microsecond, there is virtually no encounter of any kind: there is union.[25] At that vanishingly tiny instant, any possible I-Thou encounter—indeed, any kind of over-againstness at all—is held in abeyance.

All cognitive encounters have at least a trace of this recurring moment, of course, but we may take what Tillich says about religious encounter as illustrative, since religious encounter has a maximum of this moment. In such knowing, the union of subject and object is so pronounced that over-againstness virtually disappears. In such knowing, "participation . . . means being grasped on a level of one's own reality and of reality generally which is not determined by the subject-object structure of finitude, but which underlies this structure" (MW 1:388).

But now, as we begin to slide our finger gradually up the curved line of increasing separation, we find that we are not moving any closer to a potential I-Thou encounter, and that we never will move any closer—not on this line. Rather, we are moving into moments of stronger and stronger separation and objectification; and such moments are quite different from moments of I-Thou relatedness (in the Buberian sense I am working with).

---

[25]Of course, this is not to say Tillich rules out "encounter." It is a perfectly appropriate use of language when he speaks of the succession of alternating moments *as a whole*—as a whole that includes both extremes—as an "encounter."

The problem is that there are only two axes in Tillich's model. We need a third axis—not just "forward," and not just "up and down," but now also "from side to side." We need an axis on which we could plot periods of I-It activity "to the left," let us say, and periods of I-Thou engagement "to the right." Thus equipped, we could say that at the same time our experience is unfolding "forward" through time, and oscillating "up and down" in the separating/participating way, it is alternating "from side to side" between periods of I-It activity and periods of I-Thou engagement—the two possibilities Buber discusses.[26]

To make my emerging model more intuitively accessible, I should touch it up in one respect. As we saw in chapter 4, the up-and-down moments appear to succeed one another very rapidly—usually if not always more quickly than we can consciously notice or distinguish them. The cycle of each vibration must be a matter of a tiny microsecond.

By contrast, the oscillation "left and right" between a phase of I-It activity and an episode of I-Thou relatedness is on quite a different time scale. It would appear that I-Thou episodes, even for those who are sensitive and willing for them, take place during minutes or hours that alternate with longer stretches of the "daily I-It grind"—the grind in which, perforce, we experience and use the things around us, and even the people around us, mostly as It's.

Thus, for some purposes, we might better use our up-and-down axis to trace the way different *kinds* of cognitive encounter succeed one another in an undulating line. I refer to the different kinds of encounter Tillich distinguishes by "locating them" at the three broadly distinguishable depths already explained. We are occupied for much of a day at the relatively shallow level of controlling knowledge: there is exacting analysis to be done; there are technical problems to be solved. But the day is graciously punctuated by coffee breaks or what have you, periods of personal relatedness into which we enter at the "understanding level." And perhaps there are some moments—surely on weekends there are moments if not hours—that are imbued with an intensity that is

---

[26]Buber, *I and Thou*, 99, 52.

downright religious: we involve ourselves at the deepest, existential level.

The line representing the conscious experience I have just described will show our familiar up-and-down undulating pattern as it moves from a deeper to a shallower kind of encounter and back again. These ups and downs will be on approximately the same time scale as the side-to-side, I-Thou/I-It alternations. And that is a happy result because the deeper moments in the Tillichian sense are the ones in which possibilities for I-Thou rapport will be most likely to open up for us.

Nevertheless, my earlier microanalysis of what happens on the up-and-down axis remains extremely important, as well. It is that analysis that showed what was missing in Tillich's unimproved ontology. Especially because this graphed model is complex, however, I shall take it as a metaphor in what follows. I shall do no more than lean on it implicitly. I shall not appeal to it as such.

6. The Difference the Proposed Changes Make

As I have made clear, the main change I want to make in Tillich's ontology is to incorporate into his model of reality the missing I-Thou of Martin Buber. The place in the Tillichian model at which that kind of over-againstness would have to be added is in "the basic ontological structure," which is labeled the "self-world correlation" (ST 1:299; cf. 1:164, 168-74). Accordingly, I propose that an I-Thou vis-à-vis of this kind be added as a structural component of Tillich's self-world correlation. The added component is Buber's "a priori of relation, the inborn Thou,"[27] which was presented in section 3 above.

What is reality like according to the now-augmented Tillichian model? Given the limited room I have, I must answer that question in a highly compressed way. There are at least ten things that have to be said. I divide the ten into four categories, a–d.

a. *Human being in the world.* The first four of the ten things to be said have to do with human being in the world.

---

[27]Buber, *I and Thou*, 27, sect. 27.

(1) However much or little we actually do enter into I-Thou relations, it is part of our essential human being that we may step into *direct*, exclusive, reciprocal, I-Thou relations with some of the beings in our world. These I-Thou "others" include especially, though not solely, our fellow human beings.[28] This direct, exclusive, and reciprocal relation is not possible in Tillich (as I have argued in sections 3 and 5 above).

(2) In addition to our being able to relate to some worldly beings in this way, we also (as provided in Tillich's unaltered model) objectify and participate in these Thous, just as (in general) we objectify and participate in any other being lodged within the grid of our world. The activity in which this takes place is (in Tillich's evocative terminology) our simultaneously "shaping" and "grasping" our objects and our world, including our self as belonging to our world. The shaping takes place in the "outward" world, the grasping takes place within our "inner," mental-spiritual life (ST 1:76).

(3) And now a major "join" between the Tillichian and the Buberian scheme: our objectifying-participating, grasping-shaping intercourse with our world (so Tillich) is the same thing, in an enhanced description, as our experiencing, using, and objectifying beings as "Its," "Hes," or "Shes" (so Buber)—as unities of qualities or functions set in space-time and governed by causal laws.

(4) Where we mutually participate in others at some depth (à la Tillich), possibilities for I-Thou relations of communion with some of them are provided in the encounters we sustain with them *when and insofar as* they, by grace, offer this relation to us by speaking Thou to us *and* we are forthcoming with the attentiveness and will. Tillich's model of reality (see item 2) does not provide for this possibility.

b. *The divine-human encounter.* Further, my revised model warrants my saying three things about the divine-human encounter (items 5, 6, and 7). Except for the matter of "incarnation," Tillich and Buber largely concur on these three points.

---

[28]For want of space I do not deal with our I-Thou relations either with beings in nature or with the intelligible forms Buber calls *geistige Wesenheiten*. See Buber, *I and Thou*, 6, 9.

(5) In and through each of the worldly encounters noted in item 4, we are also confronted, though we do not usually recognize it, by the Eternal Thou, God.

(6) We cannot make the Eternal Thou who thus confronts us into an it. Neither can this Thou be domiciled or located within this world, except in terms of a paradoxical "inbreak" into our world that provides a "center" to our history (the history that defines our full human being)—a center that, at its paradigmatic fullest, is "incarnation."

The notions of "paradox" and "center of history" I have just used are employed in full-blooded Tillichian senses.[29] Although Buber comes surprisingly close to the idea of incarnation I intend,[30] one wonders whether he has the right to say all that. In any case, his Jewish categories will not accommodate all I have in mind. Hence I propose a simple but far-reaching change. It is a change I think epitomizes perhaps the most basic difference between Judaism and Christianity. Buber's principle is that the Eternal thou is "the Thou that by its nature cannot become It."[31] I propose, as a Christian alternative: God is the Thou who by its nature cannot be *made into* an It. This leaves open the possibility that, in sacraments, and paradigmatically in the incarnation, God may graciously "itify" God's own self for us.

(7) The confrontation with the Eternal Thou belongs to—and is ontologically located in—what Tillich talks about when he speaks of the inner infinity or transcendent depth of our lived world.

c. *Rendering the divine depth: adding to and diverging from Tillich.* Nevertheless, the inner infinity or divine depth of which I have just spoken is in some important respects rendered differently in

---

[29]For Tillich's subtle and profound idea of "the center of history," see pp. 131-33, 135, above. For the Tillichian notion of paradox, see pp. 42-44, above, and also my "Tillich's Dialectic," *Papers from the Annual Meeting of the North American Paul Tillich Society, Washington, D.C., 1993*, ed. Robert P. Scharlemann (Charlottesville VA: North American Paul Tillich Society, 1994) 9-17.

[30]Buber speaks of "a mixture of the divine and human" in "a new form of God in the World" that comes to pass in a revelatory event the world is mature enough to receive. Buber, *I and Thou*, 115, 61.

[31]Buber, *I and Thou*, 75, sect. 44.

our model from what one finds in Tillich himself. The main differences are two (items 8 and 9):

(8) However much or little we enter into the relation with the Eternal Thou that is "proffered" in the confrontation noted in items 5-7, that confrontation itself persists. Its ongoing over-againstness vis-à-vis each creaturely being qualifies the transcendent depth (or inner infinity) of our self and our world. This feature of the transcendent depth of life is what Buber calls "the a priori of relation, the inborn Thou," a point I have addressed above.

(9) By virtue of its Thouness, the Eternal Thou calls us into being as persons—calls us in and from out of the transcendent depths of life. Although Tillich's model includes much of what is involved at this point (see item 10), my model incorporates Buber's "inborn Thou" here, and not just Tillich's "late-born Thou" (so I label it in language I admit is polemical). By a "late-born Thou" I mean that, for Tillich, God *becomes* Thou for us. As Tillich puts it, "Certainly in the I-Thou relationship of man and *his* God, God becomes *a* being, *a* person, *a* 'thou' for us."[32]

d. *Rendering the divine depth: Tillich doctrine that is retained.* Notwithstanding the revisions of Tillich described in items 8 and 9, some things about the transcendent depth of life remain the same.

(10) In my revised model, the transcendent depths of self and world continue to be understood in the following very Tillichian ways: in or from out of that depth (a) we are posited in our essential being; (b) we are empowered to exist or to actualize ourselves; (c) we are summoned into actual being; (d) we are constrained by such unconditional norms as love, justice, truth, and expressiveness; (e) we are resisted or "judged" insofar as we are estranged and destructive distortions of our essential being; and, finally, (f)

---

[32]Paul Tillich, "Reply to Interpretation and Criticism," in *The Theology of Paul Tillich*, ed. Charles W. Kegley and Robert W. Bretall (New York: Macmillan, 1952) 341. See also Tillich, *Biblical Religion*, 26-27. There Tillich is explaining how religions East and West are *alike* in being personalistic. He quotes a Hindu's comment that "the Brahman power makes itself personal for us." *Biblical Religion*, 26. God must wait until human beings are personal to be fully personal Godself. "The God who is unconditional in power, demand, and promise is the God who makes us completely personal and who, *consequently*, is completely personal in our encounter with him." *Biblical Religion*, 27; emphasis added.

we nonetheless are accepted and graced—all this (that is, [a]-[f]), within or from out of the transcendent depth of life.

7. Conclusion

Speaking with as much seriousness as playfulness, I can say that I have written this chapter in the hope that a new species might evolve, namely, revisionist Tillichians. What would this species look like? One identifying trait is that members of this species would generally agree with the following statement Buber makes in his 1957 postscript to his 1923 classic *Ich und Du*.

> The description of God as a Person is indispensable for everyone who . . . means by "God," as I do, him who—whatever else he may be—enters into a direct relation with us men in creative, revealing and redeeming acts, and thus makes it possible for us to enter into a direct relation with him. This ground and meaning of our existence constitutes a mutuality, arising again and again, such as can subsist only between persons.[33]

With the end of this chapter, I also bring part three of the book to a close, and therewith the book as a whole. If what I have said can shed some light and give some guidance for our dealing with the interreligious relations in which we become involved, I shall be pleased. One of my two purposes in writing the book will have been fulfilled.

So far as the other main purpose I have had in mind is concerned—the scholarly one—I am struck with a final question, but also with a reassuring answer. Have I managed accurately and faithfully to render Tillich's thought? I have sometimes been rather bold, not just in this chapter, where of course I deliberately depart from Tillich, but also in other chapters, where I have sought to work out the implications and draw upon the possibilities of what he had to say.

But the reassuring answer that comes back can be expressed in an utterly fictional response that Tillich himself might make to my question. "It was my purpose," Tillich might say, "to challenge my readers and hearers to take what I have written and said, and to

---

[33]Buber, *I and Thou*, 124.

be driven by it and through it to something creative, something
deep, something that will illumine, enliven, and make meaningful
the time and place in which they find themselves."

I hope I have been able to do that.

Bibliography of Sources Cited

Published Works of Paul Tillich

"Art and Ultimate Reality." In Paul Tillich, *On Art and Architecture*, edited by John Dillenberger and Jane Dillenberger, 139-57. New York: Crossroad, 1989.

Biblical Religion and Ultimate Reality. Chicago: University of Chicago Press, 1955.

Christianity and the Encounter of the World Religions. New York and London: Columbia University Press, 1963. Also, *Christianity and the Encounter of World Religions*. Foreword by Krister Stendahl. With an added appendix: "The Significance of the History of Religions for the Systematic Theologian" (12 October 1965—Tillich's last public lecture; see below). Fortress Texts in Modern Theology. Minneapolis: Fortress Press, 1994. I regularly cite both editions.

The Courage to Be. New Haven and London: Yale University Press, 1952.

"Dimensions, Levels, and the Unity of Life." *Kenyon Alumni Bulletin* (Kenyon College, Gambier OH) (October-December 1958): 4-8.

Dynamics of Faith. New York, Evanston, and London: Harper & Row, 1957. Also in a Perennnial Classics Edition. Introduction by Marion Pauck. New York: Perennial/HarperCollins Publishers, 2001.

The Encounter of Religions and Quasi-Religions. Edited by Terence Thomas. Lewiston NY/Queenston Ontario/Lampeter Wales: Edwin Mellen Press, 1990.

Ergänzungs- und Nachlassbände zu den Gesammelte Werke. Volume 2. Edited by Renate Albrecht. Stuttgart: Evangelisches Verlagswerk, 1972.

The Essential Tillich. Edited by F. Forrester Church. New York: Collier-Macmillan, 1987.

"Existential Analyses and Religious Symbols." In *Four Existentialist Theologians*, edited by Will Herberg, 277-91. Garden City NY: Doubleday Anchor Books/Doubleday and Company, 1958.

Gesammelte Werke. Edited by Renate Albrecht. Fourteen volumes. Stuttgart: Evangelisches Verlagswerk, 1959–1990. (Cited as GW in texts and notes above.)

The Interpretation of History. Translated by N. A. Rasetzki and Elsa L. Talmey. New York: Charles Scribner's Sons, 1936.

"Japan, 1960: Paulus Writes." In Hannah Tillich. *From Place to Place*, 93-114. New York: Stein and Day, 1976.

"Jewish Influences on Contemporary Christian Theology." *Cross Currents* 2/3 (1952): 34-42.

Love, Power, and Justice. New York: Oxford University Press, 1954.

Main Works / Hauptwerke. Edited by Carl Heinz Ratschow with the collaboration of John Clayton, Gert Hummel, Erdmann Sturm, Michael Palmer, Robert P. Scharlemann, and Gunther Wenz. Six volumes. Berlin and New York: De Gruyter—Evangelisches Verlagswerk GmbH, 1987–1998. (Cited as MW in the text and notes above.)

"Missions and World History." *The Theology of the Christian Mission*, edited by Gerald H. Anderson, 281-89. New York: McGraw-Hill, 1961.

My Search for Absolutes. Credo Perspectives. Edited by Ruth Nanda Anshen. New York: Simon & Schuster, 1967.

Perspectives on 19th and 20th Century Protestant Theology. Edited and with an introduction by Carl E. Braaten. New York, Evanston, and London: Harper & Row, 1967. London: SCM Press, 1967.

The Protestant Era. Translated by James Luther Adams. Chicago: University of Chicago Press, 1948.

"Reinhold Niebuhr's Doctrine of Knowledge." In *Reinhold Niebuhr: His Religious, Social, and Political Thought*, edited by Charles W. Kegley and Robert W. Bretall, 36-43. New York: Macmillan, 1956.

"A Reinterpretation of the Doctrine of the Incarnation." *Church Quarterly Review* (London) 147 (1949): 135-148.

The Religions Situation. Translated by H. Richard Niebuhr. New York: Living Age Books/Meridian Books, 1956. Originally published in 1932 by Henry Holt & Company.

"Reply to Interpretation and Criticism." In *The Theology of Paul Tillich*, edited by Charles W. Kegley and Robert W. Bretall, 329-49. New York: Macmillan, 1952.

The Shaking of the Foundations. New York: Charles Scribner's Sons, 1948.

"The Significance of the History of Religions for the Systematic Theologian." Appendix in Paul Tillich, *Christianity and the Encounter of World Religions* (see above), foreword by Krister Stendahl, 63-79. Fortress Texts in Modern Theology. Minneapolis: Fortress Press, 1994. This was Tillich's last public lecture (12 October 1965). It was recorded on tape and edited by Jerald C. Brauer for the posthumous volume *The Future of Religions* (New York: Harper & Row, 1966). It was reprinted in *Theological Writings*, 431-46, and in *Main Works/Hauptwerke* 6, and finally included as an appendix to the 1994 work cited here.

Systematic Theology. Three volumes. Chicago: University of Chicago Press, 1951, 1957, 1963. (Cited as ST in the text and notes above.) Also: Welwyn, England: J. Nisbet, 1964. Three volumes in one: Chicago: University of Chicago Press, 1967.

The Theology of Culture. New York: Oxford University Press, 1959.

What Is Religion? Edited with an introduction by James Luther Adams. Translated by James Luther Adams and Charles W. Fox. New York: Harper & Row, 1969.

Unpublished Works of Paul Tillich

"The Present Encounter of World Religions." Wesley Lecture delivered in Chapel Hill, North Carolina, 3 October 1958. Notes by Robison B. James in his personal files.

"The Present Encounter of Religious and Secular Faiths." Wesley Lecture delivered in Chapel Hill, North Carolina, 4 October 1958. Notes by Robison B. James in his personal files.

Secondary Sources

Ahlstrom, Sydney E. A *Religious History of the American People*. New Haven: Yale University Press, 1972.

Albanese, Catherine L. *America: Religions and Religion*. Belmont CA: Wadsworth Publishing Co., 1981.

Anderson, Bernhard W., and Katheryn Pfisterer Darr. *Understanding the Old Testament*. Abridged fourth edition. Upper Saddle River NJ: Prentice-Hall, 1998.

Anselm, Saint. *Proslogium; Monologium; An Appendix on Behalf of the Fool by Gaunilon; and Cur Deus Homo*. Translated by Sidney Norton Deane. La Salle IL: Open Court Publishing Company, 1961.

Bayer, Oswald. *Theologie. Handbuch Systematischer Theologie*. Edited by Carl Heinz Ratschow. Volume 1. Gütersloh: Gütersloher Verlagshaus, 1994.

Boss, Marc. "*Coincidentia oppositorum* und Rechtfertigung—das cusanische Erbe in Paul Tillichs Denken." *Mystisches Erbe in Tillichs philosophischer Theologie, Beiträge des VIII. Internationalen Paul-Tillich-Symposiums, Frankfurt/Main 2000*, edited by Gert Hummel and Doris Lax, 135-63. *Tillich-Studien* 3. Edited by Werner Schüssler and Erdmann Sturm. Münster/Hamburg/London: LIT-Verlag, 2000.

Boyd, Gregory A., and Paul R. Eddy. *Across the Spectrum: Understanding Issues in Evangelical Theology.* Grand Rapids MI: Baker Book House, 2002.

Brown, Robert McAfee, editor. *Kairos: Three Prophetic Challenges to the Church.* Grand Rapids MI: Eerdmans, 1990.

_____. *Liberation Theology: An Introductory Guide.* Louisville KY: Westminster/John Knox Press, 1993.

Buber, Martin. *I and Thou.* Second British edition with a postscript by the author. Translated by Ronald Gregor Smith. Edinburgh: T. & T. Clark, 1959; ©1958. USA second edition: New York: Scribner's, 1958; Scribner Classics edition, 2000.

_____. *I and Thou. A New Translation with a Prologue "I and You" and Notes.* Translated and edited by Walter Kaufmann. New York: Charles Scribner's Sons, 1970.

_____. *Ich und Du.* In Martin Buber, *Die Schriften über das Dialogische Prinzip,* 5-121. Heidelberg: Verlag Lambert Schneider, 1954.

Calvin, John. *Institutes of the Christian Religion.* Edited by John T. McNeill. Translated by Ford Lewis Battles et al. Library of Christian Classics 21. Philadelphia: Westminster Press, 1960.

Comstock, Gary L. "Two Types of Narrative Theology." *Journal of the American Academy of Religion* 55 (Winter 1987): 687-717.

D'Costa, Gavin. *Theology and Religious Pluralism.* Oxford: Blackwell, 1986.

DiNoia, J. A. *The Diversity of Religions.* Washington DC: Catholic University of America, 1992.

Eck, Diana L. *Encountering God.* Boston: Beacon Press, 1993.

_____. *A New Religious America: How a "Christian Country" Has Now Become the World's Most Religiously Diverse Nation.* San Francisco: HarperSanFranciso, 2001.

_____. *The Pluralism Project.* Diana L. Eck, Director. Home page: <http://www.fas.harvard.edu/~pluralism/index.html>. Accessed 26 August 2002.

Grau, Karin. "Salvation as Cosmic Healing in Tillich." *North American Paul Tillich Society Newsletter* 28/3 (Summer 2002): 24-27.

Grenz, Stanley J. *Theology for the Community of God.* Grand Rapids MI: Eerdmanns, 2000.

Gutiérrez, Gustavo. "Revelation and Theological Method." In *Gustavo Gutiérrez: Essential Writings,* edited by James B. Nickoloff, 49-53. Minneapolis: Fortress Press, 1996.

_____, "Truth and Theology." In *Gustavo Gutiérrez: Essential Writings,* edited by James B. Nickoloff, 53-60. Minneapolis: Fortress Press, 1996.

Hammond, Guy B. "Tillich on the Personal God." *Journal of Religion* 46 (1964): 289-93.

Hauerwas, Stanley, and L. Gregory Jones, editors. *Why Narrative?* Grand Rapids MI: Eerdmans, 1989.

Harvey, Van A. *A Handbook of Theological Terms*. New York: Simon and Schuster, 1964.

Heschel, Abraham. *The Prophets*. New York and Evanston: Harper & Row, 1962.

Hick, John. *An Interpretation of Religion*. New Haven CT and London: Yale University Press, 1989.

_____. "The Non-Absoluteness of Christianity." In *The Myth of Christian Uniqueness*, edited by John Hick and Paul F. Knitter, 16-36. Maryknoll NY: Orbis Books, 1987.

Heim, S. Mark. *Salvations*. Maryknoll NY: Orbis, 1995.

Hopkins, Jasper. *Nicholas of Cusa's Dialectical Mysticism*. Minneapolis: Arthur J. Banning Press, 1988.

James, Robison B. "Mystical Identity and Acceptance 'In Spite Of': Paul Tillich as a Synthesis of Cusanus and Luther." *Mystisches Erbe in Tillichs philosophischer Theologie, Beiträge des VIII. Internationalen Paul-Tillich-Symposiums, Frankfurt/Main 2000*, edited by Gert Hummel and Doris Lax, 164-76. *Tillich-Studien* 3. Edited by Werner Schüssler and Erdmann Sturm. Münster, Hamburg, London: LIT-Verlag, 2000.

_____. "La rencontre interreligieuse d'après Paul Tillich: pour une nouvelle conception de l'exclusivism, de l'inclusivism et du pluralisme." Translated by Jean Richard. *Laval Philosophique et Theologique* (Québec City) 58 (2002): 43-64.

_____. "Revising Tillich's Model of Reality to Add Buber's I-Thou." In *Being versus Word in Tillich's Theology? Proceedings of the VII. International Paul-Tillich-Symposium held in Frankfurt/Main 1998*, edited by Gert Hummel, 237-47. Berlin and New York: Walter de Gruyter, 1999.

_____. "Revising Tillich's Model of Reality to Let God Be Personal." *North American Paul Tillich Society Newsletter* 25/2 (Spring 1999): 5-12.

_____. "Tillich on 'the Absoluteness of Christianity'." *Papers from the Annual Meeting of the North American Paul Tillich Society, Philadelphia PA, November 1995*, edited by Robert P. Scharlemann, 35-50. Charlottesville VA: North American Paul Tillich Society, 1997.

_____. "Tillich's Dialectic." In *Papers from the Annual Meeting of the North American Paul Tillich Society, Washington DC, 1993*, edited by Robert P. Scharlemann, 9-17. Charlottesville VA.: North American Paul Tillich Society, 1994.

Knitter, Paul F. *No Other Name?* Maryknoll NY: Orbis, 1985.

Macquarrie, John. "Christianity and Other Faiths." *Union Seminary Quarterly Review* 20 (November 1964): 39-48.

_____. "Commitment and Openness." *Theology Digest* 27 (Winter 1979): 347-55.

Nickoloff, James B. "Introduction." In *Gustavo Gutiérrez: Essential Writings*, edited by James B. Nickoloff, 1-22. Minneapolis: Fortress Press, 1996.

Otto, Rudolf. *The Idea of the Holy: An Inquiry into the Non-Rational Factor in the Idea of the Divine and Its Relation to the Rational*. Translated by John W. Harvey (from *Das Heilige*, 1917). New York: Oxford University Press, 1923; second edition, 1950.

Pauck, Wilhelm and Marion. *Paul Tillich: His Life and Thought*. Volume 1, *Life*. New York, Hagerstown, San Francisco, London: Harper & Row, 1976.

Pinnock, Clark H. *A Wideness in God's Mercy: The Finality of Jesus Christ in a World of Religions*. Grand Rapids MI: Zondervan, 1992.

Putnam, Hilary. *Reason, Truth, and History*. Cambridge: Cambridge University Press, 1981.

Race, Alan. *Christians and Religious Pluralism*. Maryknoll NY: Orbis, 1982.

Ratschow, Carl Heinz. "Einführung." In *Tillich-Auswahl*, volume 1, edited by Manfred Baumotte, 10-100. Gütersloh: Gütersloher Verlagshaus Mohn, 1980.

Rescher, Nicholas. *The Strife of Systems*. Pittsburgh: University of Pittsburgh Press, 1985.

Richardson, Alan, and John Bowden, editors. *The Westminster Dictionary of Theology*. Philadelphia: Westminster Press, 1983.

Sanders, John. *No Other Name: An Investigation into the Destiny of the Unevangelized*. Grand Rapids MI: Eerdmans, 1992.

Schuon, Frithjof. *The Transcendent Unity of Religions*. Revised edition. Translated by Peter Townsend with an introduction by Huston Smith. New York: Harper & Row, 1975.

Thatamanil, John J. "Managing Multiple Religious and Scholarly Identities." *Journal of the American Academy of Religion* 68 (December 2000): 791-803.

Theunissen, Michael. *The Other: Studies in the Social Ontology of Husserl, Heidegger, Sartre, and Buber*. Translated by Christopher Macann with an introduction by Fred R. Dallmayr. Cambridge MA: MIT Press, 1984.

Thomas, Owen C. "Christianity and the Perennial Philosophy." *Theology Today* 43/2 (1986): 259-66.

_____. "Religious Plurality and Contemporary Philosophy: A Critical Survey." *Harvard Theological Review* 87 (1994): 197-213

Thomas, Terence Thomas. "Convergence and Divergence in a Plural World." In *Paul Tillich's Theological Legacy: Spirit and Community*, edited by Frederick J. Parrella, 19-42. Berlin and New York: Walter de Gruyter, 1995.

_____. *Paul Tillich and World Religions*. Fairwater, Cardiff, Wales: Cardiff Academic Press, 1999.

Troeltsch, Ernst. *The Absoluteness of Christianity and the History of Religions*. Translated by David Reid with an ntroduction by James Luther Adams. Richmond, Virginia: John Knox Press, 1971.

_____. "The Place of Christianity among the World Religions." In *Attitudes Toward Other Religions: Some Christian Interpretations*, edited by Owen C. Thomas, 73-91. New York: Harper and Row, 1969.

Tweed, Thomas A. "On Moving Across: Translocative Religion and the Interpreter's Position." *Journal of the Academy of Religion* 70 (2002): 25-77.

Wittgenstein, Ludwig. *Philosophical Investigations: The English Text of the Third Edition*. Translated by G. E. M. Anscombe. New York: Macmillan, 1958.

Unpublished Secondary Sources

Dourley, John. "Toward a Salvageable Tillich: The Implications of His Late Confesion of Provincialism." Paper presented at the annual meeting of the North American Paul Tillich Society, Toronto, Canada, November 2002.

James, Robison B. "How Postmodernism, Even Tillich, Can Help Evangelicals." Paper presented at the Third Annual Wheaton Theology Conference, Wheaton College, Wheaton, Illinois, April 1994.

_____. "The Modern Super-Acts Worldview." Self-published text in Christian Theology II, HT 2312, Baptist Theological Seminary at Richmond (Virginia). Spring semester 2002.

_____. Letter of 22 June 1997 to Carl Heinz Ratschow. In the personal files of Robison B. James.

_____. "Reconciling Hermeneutics Right and Left in American Christianity by Dissolving the 'Conspiracy' between Newtonian and Book-of-Acts Ontologies." Paper scheduled for delivery at the annual meeting of the American Academy of Religion, Southeastern division, Chattanooga, Tennessee, March 2003.

_____. "The Symbolic Knowledge of God in the Theology of Paul Tillich." Ph.D. dissertation, Duke University, 1965. UMI Dissertation Services, 300 N. Zeeb Road, Ann Arbor MI 48106.

Pinnock, Clark H. "Acts 4:12: No Other Name under Heaven." Paper presented in Edinburgh, Scotland, June 2002. In the personal files of Robison B. James.

Index of Names and Subjects